Less Stuff

More Life

Practical help for the those who desire more out of life

By Amy Maryon

Less Stuff More Life: Practical help for those who desire more out of life

Uncopyrighted 2015

Photo attribution to Benny Marty www.123rf.com

Printed in the United States of America

This book is uncopyrighted. As with all my work, I operate on the honor system and pray that my readers do the same. If you do copy my information for the encouragement of others, please provide the source and ordering information. Thank you.

Published by Create space an Amazon company

For other books by this author visit:

www.plainandnotsoplain.com

Table of Contents

chapter 1: The change: Stop wishing thing were different 11

chapter 2: The change: Eating breakfast.. 15

chapter 3: The change: Lowering your voice 19

chapter 4: The change: Drink more water 21

chapter 5: The change: clean a drawer.. 25

chapter 6: The change: Do not eat out this week 27

chapter 7: The change: choosing to have a heart of gratitude. 31

chapter 8: The change: forgiveness 35

chapter 9: The change: choosing to smile and laugh more.. 37

chapter 10: The change: to get more sleep 41

chapter 11: The change: to switch to all natural cleaners 43

chapter 12: The change: Preparing for your day... 45

chapter 13: The change: to eat more veggies and fruits... 49

chapter 14: The change: to watch your words 53

chapter 15: The change: to go TV free for 1 week 57

chapter 16: The change: to exercise 59

chapter 17: The change: clear a counter 63

chapter 18: The change: to play more 65

chapter 19: The change: to live paper and plastic free 67

chapter 20: The change: choosing to be happy 71

chapter 21: The change: to be thankful 75

chapter 22: The change: To write a letter... 77

chapter 23: The change: to take a daily vitamin. 79

chapter 24: The change: to gather up your fragments 81

chapter 25: The change: to pray.. 83

chapter 26: The change: to clean a closet 87

chapter 27: The change: To eat popcorn for a snack 91

chapter 28: The change: to praise your spouse and/or children: 93

chapter 29: The change: to let go of guilt 95

chapter 30: The change: to bake a treat this week 99

chapter 31: The change: to bless others 101

chapter 32: The change: to get rid of paper clutter 103

chapter 33: The change: to clear your inbox 105

chapter 34: The change: to plan a week of simple dinners. 107

chapter 35: The change: to listen to uplifting positive music for a week 111

chapter 36: The change: to learn to say, NO! 113

chapter 37: The change: to simplify your eating habits. 115

chapter 38: The change: to pay off small debt 119

chapter 39: The change: a place for everything 121

chapter 40: The change: to learn how to unwind from a stress filled day 123

chapter 41: The change: get back to beliefs 125

chapter 42: The change: to edit your commitments 129

chapter 43: The change: to simplify your clothing 133

chapter 44: The change: to learn calmness in ALL situations in life 135

chapter 45: The change: to subtract people/things that deduct from your life 137

chapter 46: The change: to get rid of the "bad" stuff from our diets. 141

chapter 47: The change : to challenge yourself 145

chapter 48: The change: to avoid materialism 147

chapter 49: The change: to establish routines 149

chapter 50: The change: to declutter a room 151

chapter 51: The change: Learn to let go 153

chapter 52: The change: to make small gradual changes 157

Intro

Living a simplified life has different meanings for everyone. My simple life means:

- getting rid of all but the essentials
- choosing to eliminate chaos for peace
- spending time doing what is important to me

Your definition may be different than mine, but we all have a common meaning. That meaning is we work to get rid of the many things that we do that are unproductive and wasting our days. This includes spiritual, physical, and emotional clutter which makes chaos in our life. We will then be left with the things that have value to us. This will allow us to spend time with the people we love and do the things that we love to do.
 This book will give you 52 changes to help you live a simplistic lifestyle with less stuff for more life.

 Why 52 changes? This is good to introduce something new to your life every week for a year.   Something small, but enough that you would notice if it was making a difference in your life. You may choose to do all 52 changes and that is great! Some you might choose to do and others you might not want to change. The point is to start making baby steps towards simplistic change in your life.

It can be done, in small baby steps. Sometimes you will take two steps forward and one step back. The key is to continue onward and make these changes, little by little.   Take the journey and choose to live your life plain and simple with LESS STUFF so that you can enjoy MORE LIFE.

Chapter 1

The change: Stop wishing thing were different

You might look at a person and see all the "freedoms" that they have in their life and "wish" that you had those freedoms too. Maybe you might wish you had a nicer home, more money, or a different husband—if you were going through a tough time. There are many things that we can covet and wish were different. I could go on and on about things that I "coveted" in my lifetime. Some you could agree with me that I had a right to have and other things you might think they were silly.

But that all changed. Not that I gave up "dreaming." But I gave up on the idea of wishing for things that were not a part of my life and I started being thankful for the little things.

In our lives if we stop looking at what we don't have, we might be surprised at what we do have.

When we visited Amish families, they taught me something about being content. What I noticed is that it didn't matter what types of homes the people lived in, it was the hospitality they showed that was inviting. We did visit some homes that were quite extravagant. To be honest, the fellowship was much sweeter in the homes that the home was not in a great standard of living. I don't mean that disrespectfully, the one home that we stayed in was in need of great repair, it had many things that I probably would be insistent that my husband fix immediately. But it did not matter. The wife was very content and kept her home as best as she could without feeling embarrassed by the looks of it. She portrayed a sense of humbleness that was inspiring. It made me think twice before I complained about the things that I did not have.

Why make the change:

When we look at life wishing things were different we will constantly live with a sense of conflict. When we have conflict it creates stress. When we have stress it makes us agitated.

When we are agitated we usually are angry with those around us. All that is never good. We are wanting to simplify our lives. We need to stop thinking about the physical and relationship things that we don't have and just start living. We need to focus our concentration on changing the things that we do have: whether that be a broken relationship, a home that is not so pretty, or a body that is in need of exercise. All things in life take time and energy. You need to start focusing on the right things instead of living life wishing things were different.

How do we do that:

Start today by making a list. Make a list of all of the things that you wish you had different in your life. This list might get quite long, depending on how content you are. The key is getting something of tangibleness that you can physically refer to and start making slow changes to achieving your contentedness. This was a list that I had made years ago as I was learning to simplify my life:

What I wish was different in my life:

1. Wish my home looked prettier.
2. Wish I had a different body.
3. Wish my children would stop screaming so much.
4. Wish my husband and I were closer.
5. Wish I had time for things I enjoy doing.

When I started feeling the "woe is me" syndrome I had to jump out of that instantly. I wrote everything down that I wanted changed in my life and then started devising a plan to change those things.

> **What I wish was different in my life----My plan to change:**
>
> 1. Wish my home looked prettier.
>   a. Paint rooms
>   b. Make decorations
> 2. Wish I had a different body.
>   a. Drink more water
>   b. Exercise
>   c. Change food choices
> 3. Wish my children would stop screaming so much.
>   a. Begin training sessions to teach them self-control
> 4. Wish my husband and I were closer.
>   a. Begin praying daily for husband
>   b. Begin by designating a date night each month
>   c. Choosing to do one thing for him special each day
> 5. Wish I had time for things I enjoy doing.
>   a. schedule 30 minutes for myself each day

I started the change with one item. I worked on my home. At nap time I would begin painting a room each week. I then found some creative DIY things to decorate with and made those. Yes, it took some time, but I did it.

After having many babies, I was not happy with the way my body looked so I decided to change. I lost 80 lbs. I started drinking more water, I exercised each day, and then I changed my diet. I added new things each week. It was minor at first, but over time and within a year, I had dropped all those pounds and felt great!

After I felt like I could do more I began working on more items from my list and it goes on and on…….

All these things took time, I did not do them all in one day, or even all in one week. But I started with one and added as I could. I had my list and started marking off the things that I wanted to improve upon in my life.

Contentment is influenced by external circumstances, but it is an internal attitude and can be cultivated no matter what our situation in life is. We need to stop wishing for things that we don't have and focus our attention on making the things that we do have better.

Chapter 2

The change: Eating breakfast

Breakfast is probably one of your most important meals of the day. After waking up in the morning your body has been "fasting" from food for the last 12 hours. If you skip a meal and wait to eat until lunchtime your body is deprived of those nutrients and energy. When you go to eat your next meal, your body holds onto those nutrients longer because it has been denied of them so long. Instead of burning off and using the energy to make you feel better, it simply is trying to undo the denial damage you have done to your body.

Why make the change:

1. It revs up your metabolism

Eating breakfast is a great way to "kick start" your metabolism for the day. When your body receives food in the morning, it tells your brain to "get going" and this makes your metabolism start working for the day. When you don't have breakfast, your body thinks that it needs to conserve its energy because it isn't getting any more through nutrition. This can actually slow down your metabolism which will result in burning less calories.

2. It keeps you in a good mood

By eating breakfast in the morning it does a number of things to help your mood stay bright for the day.

1. Since your body won't be starving, it is easier to get in a good mood and stay that way.
2. Provides plenty of needed energy to help you get through regular tasks for your day–which in turn can make your mood optimistic.
3. Helps regulate your blood sugar through lunch time, which plays a huge role in your mood.

3. It keeps you from binge eating

By not eating breakfast in the morning, may save you some calories for the moment, but it sets you up for failure for the rest of your day. When you deny your body food, you start feeling hungry and grumpy early in the day. By the time lunch rolls around, you are more than likely going to choose something high in fat and calories to satisfy your food cravings, because you feel so ravenous. If you can hold off through dinner without eating, chances are you will feel an overwhelming urge to snack all night, which will in turn pack on the pounds!

How do we do that:

When I was visiting the Amish homes, these women would get up early and make large complete breakfasts for their family. Most would consist of oatmeal, eggs, toast, and fruit. It was simple and basic but a good, filling meal. I didn't notice many cereal boxes strewn about the table.

I know for myself personally, having had many little ones breakfast time is not a good time for me. I had to do something quick and easy. I came out with feeding my children boxed cereal every day. It served its purpose, I was able to feed many of them quickly. But by the time an hour and a half went by they were hungry, ready for a snack.

I have since made a choice to start feeding my children oatmeal everyday for breakfast. It takes just about the same amount of time and is far better for them then boxed cereal. And do you know what? I can feed them breakfast and they don't even eat until lunchtime, three hours later. Sometimes the 3- year old will get a small snack, but for the most part they make it until lunch time.

For my own self, I never ate breakfast. When I was pregnant, I would force myself to have something. Usually toast and yogurt. But it was not something I enjoyed. I still today could go without it, but I have to choose to eat it because I see how much better I feel throughout my day. When I started my weight loss, I ate oatmeal every day for breakfast. I was amazed at how much quicker I was able to lose weight and keep it off by eating this breakfast. Oatmeal is a plain and simple food that fills you up quickly.

For someone that doesn't eat breakfast I would recommend starting small. I used to get a sick feeling after eating breakfast as my body was not used to it. To fix this, I would recommend eating just a muffin or a piece of fruit. Move up to oatmeal, I promise anyone can get used to any flavor it just takes time:) Smoothies are a great thing to make and take—we like these in the summer. Yogurt and fruit sauce are another good choice.

I would save the bacon and eggs for a treat. The eggs I would do, but for myself that takes more time. I used to hard-boil, chop, and put them on toast with cheese sprinkled for a good protein filled breakfast while pregnant. Skip any kind of processed foods or high in fat foods. Think plainer, more basic foods. A great on the go breakfast is a banana.

Remember start small, gradually move up each day to something with sustenance. Take note of how your mood is for the day, how much less you eat in a day, and maybe how you have lost a few pounds.

Chapter 3

The change: Lowering your voice

In our home, there are lots of little children. Some days there is much crying, whining, and loudness just because there are so many tiny ones. It seems there is someone who is always thirsty, grumpy, had a toy taken away, or just feels like exerting their voice. It can be very loud. I have in the past resorted to yelling to make sure that people hear me. The problem with that, is that sometimes I would "lose it" and yell because I was angry. For most of the time it was not pleasant, just loud. I was not liking this mother that "lost it" occasionally, I wanted to change.

While visiting the Amish homes, I never noticed a Mother yell at her child to come to her. In fact, most of the time they talked quietly to their children. It seems their children were "on alert" to hear Mom's voice and respond when she wanted them. I was liking that.

Why make the change:

When you have to yell to get people's attention, it shows a lack of control. It seems we "yell" to get our children to listen. Like, "Oh, Mom really means it this time because she is yelling!" But what we need to be doing is training our children to listen always, so that you do not have to "resort" to yelling.

Yelling shows a spirit that is out of control. It is a sign of stress and fatigue. If you yell to get someone's attention in the home more than likely your child will do it as well. We want to create a peaceful haven for our homes. A place where it is warm and inviting, not loud and chaotic. The first way to do that is to change the atmosphere.

How do we do that:

I know that in our home, the first day that I did this, it didn't matter. My children were still loud. Meals were loud and it was unbearable to all sit in the same "echoed" dining room. I resorted to raising my voice to tell them to be quieter. Sounds funny, you raise the voice and be the example but meanwhile they are not supposed to be loud?!?!?!? Are you seeing a bad pattern here?

What I then did is the complete opposite—-I lowered my voice, almost to a whisper. The first day I did this my children thought I was weird. The second day, they stopped and started to "tune" into what I was trying to speak to them in my whisper voice.

By the third day, I was quietly correcting them to speak quieter. Meals suddenly became enjoyable. As we were sitting around the table eating, and as the "louder" child started to speak, I quietly and gently reminded them to lower their voice. I had to do it a few times, but for the most part they learned to be quieter.

The youngest would make loud baby noises and I would immediately turn to him in a quiet, but firm voice and let him know that we do not scream like that. It is a quick discipline, done immediately to let him know it is not acceptable. This takes time, but he did learn. Now meals have become an enjoyable time to sit and eat together.

Pay attention to your "triggers." What "sets you off" to start yelling? Maybe it is a teenage child who doesn't do their homework first. Maybe it is your little ones as they make a mess over and over in your home. Whatever the "trigger" be prepared next time. Talk with your teenager before and let them know what you expect out of them as far as doing their school work. Baby proof your home to avoid messes all day long.
 There are many avenues of change you can make to help "de-stress" your life and make it more peaceful. Notice the trigger and then remove it.

Chapter 4

The change: Drink more water

For years, I would deal with nonstop headaches and lower back pain. I would reach for the over the counter pain medicine and it became a regular pill I would take. When I started my weight loss a few years ago, the first thing I did was to drink more water. I replaced all my soda, juices, and coffee drinks with water. I drank so much that I would have to go to the bathroom all of the time! By doing that it helped me to lose 80 pounds, not gorge on food anymore, completely stopped my headaches, and has cured my back pain. Water has become an essential staple in my life. When I am feeling sluggish, or achy I don't reach for the pain reliever or a cup of coffee first, I guzzle a glass of water.

Why make the change:

There are a myriad of health benefits from drinking water here are just a few:

- Helps promote weight loss–fills your belly up instead of eating too much food.
- When you think you are hungry you are usually just thirsty.
- Boosts immune system–you are less likely to get sick when you drink lots of water. You are constantly flushing out toxins and bacteria from your body.
- Most common cause of daytime fatigue? dehydration—guzzle some water and feel great.
- Less headaches–flushes out the toxins from your body.
- Cures back pain, prevents sprains and cramps—lubricates your joints and helps keep your muscles elastic to prevent joint pain.
- Improves skin complexion—moisturizes your skin, keeps it fresh, soft, glowing, and smooth. The best anti-aging treatment around!
- Most adults are popping pills for ailments and diseases that can be prevented from properly hydrating and flushing out toxins from their bodies.

- Makes you rich—-even if you buy bottled water, it is still cheaper than Starbucks and soft drinks.

How do we do that:

Okay, we know all the health benefits of drinking water, but how do we go about replacing our current drinks with water? You might think, "I really love my can of Diet Coke everyday and can't live without it." I would say, don't drop it completely. Slowing start adding water to your daily routine.

For myself, I set up my "triggers" so that I know when I am supposed to drink them. I fill a 24 ounce container and I have to drink 2 before I eat lunch. I make sure to drink 2 more before I have an afternoon coffee. Then 2 more before dinner. For myself, I know that I look forward to that cup of coffee in the afternoon. If the time rolls around and I haven't had my water, I quickly guzzle my cups before I have my coffee. Same goes before I have a meal.

Set up times that you have to finish your container of water or you will not get that next thing, whether it be lunch, snack, a soda, etc. When you set a goal with a trigger it is easier to remember to drink the water. Otherwise it will sit on your counter top for the entire day.

In time, your body will start eating less food, you might even lose your cravings for your soda or other high calorie drinks. You will definitely notice that you do not need a cup of coffee to keep yourself going for the day. Plus, your body will start feeling amazing by flushing out all the toxins.

Pay attention to your "triggers." Notice when you start to feel sluggish, notice a headache coming on, or notice when you start feeling hungry. Immediately down a container of water and see the benefits almost immediately.

Ways to make water taste better:

Even though I drink a lot of water in one day, I still do not like the taste of it. For myself I add a green tea bag to my water bottle and leave it in there for the whole day. I get a nice taste to my water. Other options are:

- add a squirt of lemon juice
- squeeze a lime wedge
- add a mint leaf
- add an orange segment
- add a peppermint tea bag to your water
- add a packet of vitamin C
- for a natural detox, add 1 Tablespoon pure maple syrup and a squirt of lemon juice

How much should I drink

 Most doctors would agree to drink until your urine is a light pale color. It is rare to over hydrate yourself but you can surely under hydrate yourself. For myself, I drink a little more than half my weight in ounces. If your weight is 130 lbs drink 65 ounces of water.

Chapter 5

The change: clean a drawer

Most everyone I know has a junk drawer or multiple junk drawers. It is the drawer that you keep throwing miscellaneous items into because you do not have a set place for the items to go to. For myself, I would keep throwing items into that drawer and when the time came to look for those items, it seems I could not find them. I would then resort to purchasing it at the store. The problem is that we sometimes will turn most all of our drawers into junk drawers, never making it easy to find what it is we need to use.

Why make the change:

Having a "catch all" junk drawer makes it easy for us to be lazy. It is much easier to throw everything into a drawer to never see it again, instead of actually putting it where it belongs. We need to eliminate the junk drawer and find a place for all of those miscellaneous items. We need to adopt the rule, "A place for everything, and everything in its place." Having clean drawers will give you a sense of satisfaction. You no longer will feel like you need to "shut out" the chaotic clutter in your life. Get rid of it! Simplify and make less stress and strain on your life. Throw away the "I might use one day" items. Give away the ones you never use, and put to use the items that are "lost" in the drawers instead of buying more.

How do we do that:

Take one drawer this week and do the following:

- Dump out the drawer.
- Throw out the trash.
- Separate items that already have a place to go to like game pieces, or sewing supplies.
- Put those items away.

- Separate the remaining items into piles of similar uses- like super glue and paper clips, screwdriver and nails, etc.
- Find a drawer organizer that fits your drawer. You can use silverware compartments, or small plastic containers from the $1 store.
- Place "like" items into the compartments.
- Label the containers to help others know where to put their "junk."
- Maintain your drawer by putting it on your cleaning schedule.

If you feel like you accomplished something and that you feel better by doing this, continue onward with the rest of the drawers in your home. Focus on cleaning one a day. In a few weeks time you should have your entire home's drawers cleaned out.

Chapter 6

The change: Do not eat out this week

This may be a hard one for some to do and an easy one for others to do. I know personally I like a Starbucks coffee on the weekends with my husband. We also enjoy eating out as a family once per week. Can you imagine the amount of money that we spend on eating out with snacks and meals in a year's time? Think about the amount of groceries that we could purchase by not eating out? Or the amount of money that we would have extra to put towards paying off debt or putting towards a special purchase?

Why make the change:

Planning ahead.

I know that for our family it is sometimes easier to go through the drive thru and grab a $1 menu at McDonalds for the family. Or when we are feeling sluggish, to grab a coffee pick me up to help us through our day. But all that extra fat, calories, and sugar is doing more harm than good to our bodies. Instead of thinking "live in the moment, I gotta have this," we need to start preparing and thinking about the future.   If I know that we are going to be running into town then I need to plan ahead. If we are going to be out during mealtimes, I have to pack some sandwiches to fill their bellies. For myself, I can make a cup of coffee that I enjoy and drink that while driving around instead of purchasing one.

It takes time to make a lunch to take to work the next day. It takes time to pack a snack or even a meal for the children on our errand days. It takes time to do everything. But if you look at the long term plan, those few extra minutes that we are taking, making, and preparing a snack or meal to take, will be less than going to doctor appointments because of illness or health problems related to diet.

Saving money.

Eating out is a waste of our money. It is money that can be spent on healthful food choices. It is a waste to spend it on fast food that will cost us money immediately, and then in years to come, cost us in healthcare visits due to illnesses related to a poor diet.

If I add up the cost that we spend on Starbucks coffee in a year's time it's ridiculous. If we go two times a week–which is typical and spend on average $25 per week that times 52 weeks comes up to $1250!!! That is a nice chunk of cash that we could be saving towards something else.

The only reason that I don't save this money is because I fail to plan ahead. If I would take the mentality of planning ahead to make sure that I have a meal packed in the car, fill up my coffee thermos, then the "crave" to eat out would be much less as I would have no need for food.

How to make the change:

Make the change now. Choose to grab a healthy snack instead of eating fast food. By keeping an apple or banana in the car and snacking on that instead of French fries when needing food is a good choice. Keep your water bottle filled with refreshing water that you continuously are drinking so that you do not feel the need for a drink of soda.

If your children get snacks when in the car, save money by taking your own. We also keep a case of water bottles in the car to save on getting drinks while out.

If I know we are going to be missing a meal, we make sandwiches to take with us. . A simple quick snack is pretzels, string cheese, and apple slices. I usually have that sort of thing on hand to grab when we are headed out.

If I am doing a weight loss challenge, I will typically take a salad to eat in the car. I will bring a bag full of cut up vegetable sticks for satisfying those munchies while driving around. Even though my first thought would be to drive thru the fast food lane, if I am prepared, I can ward off bad food choices.

Chapter 7

The change: choosing to have a heart of gratitude.

How many of us know that person who complains about everything? The person that complains about the weather, complains about their spouse, complains about the cost of things, etc. The list can go on and on. Those types of people are ones that bring us down in one full swoop if we are not careful. What about our own self? Do we ever complain about things needlessly? Do we have small talk with the cashier at the grocery store and walk away from it and realize that our conversations were not uplifting? Do we get off the phone from talking with a friend and realize that our whole conversation was about how bad of a day we were having? How much of our life is spent wishing we had this or that?

Why make the change:

A grateful heart is one that finds the countless blessings of God in the seemingly mundane everyday life.

Gratitude is good for these reasons:

1. Having a heart of gratitude allows you to be happy and celebrate today. You aren't sitting around worrying about things. You are thankful for what you have and can anticipate what God has for you next.
2. Having a heart of gratitude blocks all negative emotions. It does not allow you to sit around and wallow in self pity. It does not let you dwell on the negatives in your life. It does not overwhelm you with all of the bad that is going on around you.
3. Having a heart of gratitude will make you stress resilient. If you resist stress, that is a reflection in your life, in your marriage, in how you treat people, and towards your health.
4. Having a heart of gratitude will strengthen the bonds of your relationships with people around you. People like to

be around people who are generally happy in life. No one wants to spend time with the negative person, but they do want to be around those that are happy.
5. Having a heart of gratitude will improve your self esteem. When you are thankful for your position in life, your social situation, your job situation, and for the material goods that God has given to you, you will be accepting not wanting. When you start thanking God for what you have and stop looking at what you don't have, you will become a happier person.

How to make the change:

If you find it hard to change your attitude from pessimism to optimism you need to train your heart to look for the good things in your life. Start when you first wake up in the morning, say five things you are thankful for. Speak them out loud. Eventually it will convince you to believe it. Do this a few times during your day: in the morning, at lunch, in the afternoon, and before you go to bed.

When you start to feel yourself becoming negative about something immediately change it to a positive. When your child makes a mess for the hundredth time during the day, say, "I am thankful that I have this child and that he is physically able to move and make messes like this and that I am physically able to clean it up!" Well it doesn't have to be that severe but you get the idea of being thankful for anything that can help turn around your negative thinking.

I know when I have a mountain of dishes to do, and we ALWAYS have a mountain of dishes to do, I start thanking God for the food and the ability to be able to prepare and make this food for our large family. I do know that someone, somewhere is not getting their bellies full for dinner that night.

Whenever we are faced with any type of trials or temptations, start looking for ways to be thankful for them.

Say the words, "thank you" to your spouse, or children, or whomever else you come in contact with this week. Say it more than once. Catch yourself saying it almost to the point of it being annoying to you:) Cultivate it, and the more that you say it, the more it will become part of your heart.

It's not happiness that brings us gratitude, its gratitude that brings us happiness.

Chapter 8

The change: forgiveness

Hate………..is such a strong word. Whenever you hear someone say I hate this person or that thing, it almost always emerges negative images in our brains.

What if you have someone whom you hate…maybe someone who:

- has hurt you, physically or emotionally
- has deceived you
- took a part of your pureness
- taken someone away from you

Over the course of my life I have learned that there is no hope or salvation in hatred. Hate will eat you alive. If you expect to be whole you must let go. The energy spent being angry or getting even should be better directed at something useful.

Why make the change:

Forgiveness is your first step toward a life free of hate.

What does forgiveness mean?

Forgiveness means…….

- I hate no more
- I can go to sleep at night without worrying about it
- I release my stress to someone else
- FREEDOM
- helping others
- a better world
- letting go and releasing something powerful
- a desire to grow

When you forgive you may never forget, but you allow God to heal that wound in your soul.

How to make the change:

Forgiving someone is not easy, it may take a long time to do it but in order for you to be whole again you need to forgive. When you say I forgive you to that person, it still hurts. It does take time. But in time, you are the one left not hurting anymore. I have had to endure some painful hurt in my life and one of the best things I did was to tell that person that I forgave them for what they did to me. Years later I do not have to deal with the wound anymore, it has been healed completely. I don't feel the pain I once did, the memories are there but the pain is gone. I have seen friends who have never forgiven for the same pain I endured and I saw how it just ripped apart their life. I didn't want that, and you DON'T have to have that. Even though we go through bad things in life, it doesn't mean that we have to let it ruin us. Let it make you stronger, bolder.

Are there some people in your life whom you have hatred towards? Someone that you need to forgive and move on with your life? Start today by making simple steps towards forgiveness. Forgive God for being angry at Him, forgive yourself for letting things happen, forgive others for doing you harm. Forgive and move on.

Chapter 9

The change: choosing to smile and laugh more.

After a night with no sleep and cranky children I was feeling a little "worn" today. I was sitting with my children having oatmeal for breakfast, and we were talking about our tasks for the day. Sighs and groans started to proceed out of their mouths. I wanted to stop and discipline them for being so cranky, then I had to remind myself that they learn from their Momma whom they see each and every day. I was reminded of the verse:

"Rejoice evermore!"

This is something that has been one thing I wish I would have done more of in my life. Especially when life was filled with a constant circle of nursing, changing diapers, feeding toddlers, no sleep, etc. Life was busy. Well life is always busy no matter what you do, but at that time I was just in survival mode. Most of it was a big blur. Looking back my children probably saw more of Mommy being tired, worn, and probably a little bit cranky. That is something I wanted to change.

Why make the change:

Have you checked yourself in the mirror lately? What kind of feeling are people getting from you when they see you? Are you bringing a sense of positiveness to peoples life by your smile? Or are you bringing more tense, stressful things to the room? Are people always wondering what type of "mood" you will be in next? Or are they excited to be around you?

A smile or a laugh is contagious. Being around people that are smiling and laughing will bring healing and happiness to your life. It will lower stress levels, it will turn a bad day into good. It will help change your mind set on things.

Smiles can:

- break down the cold walls of indifference

- warm a lonely heart
- influence choices of people
- brighten your mood
- improve your outlook
- help you to make positive choices in life
- give a person who is suffering, hope
- show you have a great attitude–even in mistakes and failures, it shows that you can find the humor

When we go out I try and teach my children to always smile at people. I tell them that your little smile might just change the way a person's day goes. That person might be going through a rough patch in their life and seeing you smile or laugh might just touch their heart. It may even give the "lost", a glimmer of hope in life.

My hope for them now is to see me smile more. Now that life is a little more manageable, I feel like I have a second to breathe and think about things more. It is times like this that I sit and be silly with them. I smile and kiss my babies more. I want them to remember Momma as a hard working woman who smiled when she went about her daily duties.

I want them to remember my smile.

How to make the change:

Smiles don't just happen. You can't just set it on your face and keep it there without thinking about it. You need to consciously think to smile. When things start to go bad, put on that smile. Force yourself to "fake it till you make it" By putting a smile on, laughing at your mistakes and failures, will enable you to let go of the stress of dealing with things. It will help you to put a positive spin on the situation.

When you are with people around you that are not smiling be the first one. Don't wait for someone else to initiate the smile, go for it. Show them that your smile means that you will give them the attention they deserve. It also helps bolster open body language, and reassures the other person of your sincerity. They will be more likely to open up to things when they see that you generally care and are interested.

Your smile is the greatest gift of all!

Chapter 10

The change: to get more sleep

If you are reading this and have been a mother of young children at one point in your life, than you know what it means to be sleep deprived. I don't think I have to say anymore about how it feels to not get enough sleep.

Why make the change:

I think we all know how important health wise it is to get sleep. But did you know that your lack of sleep will affect your motivation to want to change your habits in life?

Think about weight loss. If you are motivated to lose weight, you might dive into it full force and do great for a while. Then over time, children wake up a lot during the night and your sleep level goes down. The next few days while you are trying to catch up on sleep, you are more tired. When you are more tired you don't want to exercise. It is much easier to just grab some comforting food instead of taking the time to make a healthy low fat meal. You use the excuse, "I will start again next week." Then the cycle goes around and around. Your weight loss comes to a halt.

The same is true for de-cluttering your home. You might start de-cluttering and weeding out part of your home then you stay up late some nights and aren't able to catch up on sleep. That great big project you started "organizing and de-cluttering," starts becoming this monstrous thing you took upon yourself. You start looking at your project as too overwhelming. You are tired, and just give up on it as you go, sit and watch TV. You want to comfort your feelings of feeling crappy and tired so you just give up on your de-cluttering. Your strong feelings of being motivated and wanting to de-clutter your home have taken a back seat. Time for tiredness to take over.

How to make the change:

- Go to bed earlier. If you are tired and not getting enough sleep, quit staying up late. Go to bed, in a few days when your body has adjusted you will be able to go to sleep a little bit later. But for now—go to bed.
- Some of you like to wake up early and get your day started—but if you were up late into the night with a child or just couldn't sleep, then sleep in. Don't make this a regular thing but for those occasions when you could not avoid being woken up during the night then use it.
- Have a bedtime routine. For myself I like to brush my teeth, get a drink, and shut down my computer, TVs, and phone. I then lay in complete silence and have a time with the Lord.
- Do not go to bed watching TV or surfing the internet, it will only keep you awake longer at night.
- If I am having a hard time falling asleep, I think about my day and go over what I did. I like to take this time to think about what happened or what I could have changed. Use this time to pray for your children. We have many children by the time I get through them al,l I almost always am tired and will fall asleep:)

If you are having problems wanting to start any of these lifestyle changes, look at your sleep habits and evaluate whether you are getting enough or not. That may be the factor.

Chapter 11

The change: to switch to all natural cleaners

Many people these days are concerned about eating more natural foods. They might even be more concerned about what types of "unnatural" things that may be lurking in their favorite convenience foods. But are people thinking about all the chemicals that they are exposing themselves and their families to on a daily basis through household cleaners?

I know for myself, I was more concerned with food and didn't think much that my baby was crawling around on my freshly disinfected floor that I cleaned with bleach! What was I thinking?!?!?!? Now when I clean my bathrooms I can take my toddler with me and not be worried what types of fumes he is breathing while I am cleaning the tub.

Why make the change:

There are a myriad of reasons of why you should make the change to more natural cleaners. Just take one walk down the isle of cleaning products in the grocery store. The smell from the chemicals can be overwhelming. If you use any type of rust removing cleaner you know that just one splash on your hands and they are burning. Manufacturers are not required by law to put their ingredients on labels. The labels of DANGER, WARNING, and POISON only give a general idea about the substances a product contains. Let me remind you that just because a label says "natural" does not mean it is safe. Arsenic is a naturally occurring substance and yet it kills. There is no law or set of guidelines to instruct companies as to how they can or can't label products with use of the word "natural." Don't let that word persuade you, it means nothing on a commercial product.

How to make the switch:

As with everything in life, we do things in baby steps. Ten years ago, I was selling homemade all natural cleaners but then got lapse and started using store bought chemical cleaners. I had baby after baby and found it "easier" to waste my money on "convenience" cleaners. Over the last three years I really started to examine what I was doing in my life and wanted to make some changes, one of those changes was a switch to all natural cleaners. I did it in steps.

First, I made some all purpose spray, and started using that on a daily basis. It took about 2 weeks to really feel like I was getting things cleaned. This has been my favorite cleaner and I use it on everything. Lots of potty training mistakes-- it takes the urine smell right out. I use it every day in my bathrooms and it cleans them up without leaving behind soapy residue like cleaners would.

Here are some recipes for natural cleaning products that I personally use in our home:

All purpose cleaner	Wood cleaner	Window and glass cleaner
2 teaspoons castile soap 5 Tablespoons vinegar 2 teaspoons borax 1 teaspoon baking soda 4 cups hot water Tea tree oil Peppermint oil	1 cup olive oil ½ cup lemon juice	1 cup water 1 cup alcohol 1 cup vinegar 2 squirts castile soap

Place them in squirt bottles and use microfiber cloths to do your wiping with.

Your pocket book, your lungs, and your long term health will thank you for doing this.

Chapter 12

The change: Preparing for your day

As I was feeding my children breakfast, I was rushed and harried. Quickly getting a bowl of oatmeal for this child, getting a sippy cup for that child, wiping up a mess here, telling the dog to stop barking and trying to make myself a cup of coffee, my pace was fast. Stress levels were high, I was wearing my angry eyebrows, and my mind was in a million different places. I then noticed my youngest ones were sitting quietly looking at me. I realized when my mind was elsewhere I am surely missing great moments with my children today.

I stopped, took a breath, got my cup of coffee, bowl of oatmeal and sat down with my children. I changed my moment, and I changed my day. I started asking them about how they slept, what we were going to do for the day, and in an instant my craziness ended.

Instead of thinking about all the things I had to do today I started thinking what was happening right now. Right now my children and I were enjoying a moment of sharing and talking. It was truly nice.

An incident like this not only brought joy into my heart, it brought a realization into my mind. A realization that I can either have a stressed, difficult day, or I can have an amazing wonderful day. The choice was mine. That day I chose to have an amazing, wonderful day.

Why make the change:

We all know, or should know that by preparing for our mornings will help our day be more productive, keep us in a happier mood, and generally will ensure us of a "good day." I know for myself, how I begin my mornings often sets the tone and attitude for my day. It can also derail or direct my focus. If I remain committed to preparing for my days, then I am less likely to fall prey to feeling unproductive and distracted by the end of my day.

How to make the change:

1. It helps to prepare for your morning the night before. Go through your house after the children are in bed. Do a quick pick up of the floors, wash the dishes in the sink, get your coffee pot loaded for the morning, set out breakfast bowls. Do anything that will help your mornings glide smoothly.
2. Set an alarm clock and wake up the first time it goes off. Avoid the snooze button. The moment you choose to snooze, more than likely you will end up sleeping too late. Just get directly out of bed. Don't lay and turn and stretch, just get up!
3. Start your day with a large glass of water. Coffee is great for mornings. But after sleeping and not drinking anything through the night, your body is dehydrated. Squeeze a little lemon in it for some great detoxification and hydration properties.
4. Shower and get dressed for the day. Sounds fairly simple. But most moms that stay at home rarely have time to shower and will stay in their pjs all day long. Getting a refreshing shower and putting on some clothes besides sweats is a great way to say "Hey, I am ready for my day!" Even if you can't shower in the mornings, splash some cold water on your face to help waken it up.
5. Have some quiet time with the Lord before everyone wakes up. Give yourself at least a half hour of time. Some time is better than no time. If you can't start at 30 minutes, begin with 10.
6. Eat a healthy breakfast. For most moms this is overlooked, but I know firsthand how important it is to have some type of fuel in your body after a long night without any. Kick start your body by having a healthy breakfast. No time?? Grab an apple or banana, something is better than nothing.
7. You have the power to decide what kind of day you will have. If your first thoughts are negative, instantly change your thought pattern. Say 5 things you are thankful for

and think on those things. They may be as simple as, "I'm thankful for hot water to shower with, " or "food to feed my family."

By preparing for your day the night before will help you to begin on the right foot. We want to try and eliminate things in our lives that are creating chaos. If you find that your mornings do not run smoothly, I encourage you to do this change.

Chapter 13

The change: to eat more veggies and fruits

Many of us, do not eat enough fresh fruits and vegetables each day. Our diets may consist of fast food, convenience meals, and comfort snacks. Besides, who wants to munch on a dry piece of celery, or grab an apple instead of that ooey gooey chocolate chip cookie sitting on the counter? Or better yet sit down to a leafy, lifeless salad while everyone else is eating cheesy, layered lasagna? Doesn't sound very appealing does it?

Why make the change:

Why do we need to make this change? Because we NEED to make this change. Our minds have been programmed to believe that we DON"T need these healthy foods anymore. I grew up with the typical diet of MANY American children. It consisted of:

- breakfast– a toaster pop, or processed, dyed, filled-with-sugar cereal
- lunch– a bologna sandwich on white bread with mayo, and a juice box
- after school snack– a prepacked snack cake
- dinner– TV dinners

There was no "push" to eat fresh fruit and vegetables. That was something you ate when you were on a diet. It was a "chore" to eat carrot sticks and celery. Our mentality was brainwashed into thinking that this food was actually good for us.

Thank God for the internet and people's interest into "whole foods." It is surprising to some, to know foods that are as natural as the day they were picked are better for us than the ones that are marketed to us through the television and prepared in a factory to help make our lives easier.

We need to know that ANY food prepared in a facility loses its nutritional value. We need to pick foods closest to their natural state. One of the easiest things is fruits and vegetables. They take little preparing and are chocked full of nutrients.

How to make the change:

Now remember if you were a typical "junk food" person and you have no real connections with eating fruits and vegetables, know that they are not going to be very appealing at first. Your taste buds are programmed to be stimulated by salty, fried, sugar coated foods. Fruits with basic sugars are not going to be as tasty as those brownie bites sitting in your cupboard. You need to reprogram your taste buds and brain into eating this "basic" tasting food. It will take some time, but I know that I really enjoy the taste of fruits and look forward to my daily salad with all its different vegetable toppings. At first it was just lettuce topped with dressing to smother it, but now it is a minimal amount of dressing and different fruits and vegetables to flavor the lettuce.

I would suggest that you make sure that you always have a bowl of fruit in your refrigerator. If it is something that needs preparation like grapes or watermelon, make sure it is prepared. We keep a bowl of apples and oranges filled in the refrigerator at all times. In the summer months, we always have a big fruit bowl cut up in the refrigerator.

I keep chopped up vegetables in the refrigerator for a quick snack throughout the day. If I am feeling the need to grab snacks, I place out my bowl of carrots and celery and eat that. Chewing something that has a satisfying crunch will help the munchies go away.

Whenever I purchase vegetables I try and prepare them immediately. That way it will be easier to just grab whenever I need them instead of the excuse that I don't want to have to take the time to get them out.

I usually shop once per week to ensure fresh vegetables. I prepare the ones that are going to go bad first so that we can eat those in 1-3 days and then I make the next vegetable or fruit to be prepared for the second half of the week. For example I might get cucumbers and carrots, I know that the cucumbers will go bad first so I chop those up to munch on during the first part of the week and save the carrots, which will last longer for the second half of the week. By doing this I will always have fresh veggies on hand.

If you are still drawn in to eating your processed snacks, make it a goal to eat 10 carrot sticks before you eat those snacks. I know when I was going through my weight loss, I would gorge on large amounts of vegetables cut up. But now I can just eat a few every day. I don't feel the need to fill my face anymore. I reprogrammed my brain into not eating so much. You can too.
 Help your body feel better by giving it the nutrients it deserves.

Chapter 14

The change: to watch your words

Authors note:

My apologies goes out to anyone who will read this, I did not want to type up "bad" words but I did want to bring to light those words that people might question whether they should use them. I apologize for offending anyone. I am here to help, not to judge, only share with what I feel are words of contradicting nature. Not for everyone, just for myself.

This was something that I was unaware of when I started my Christian walk. I talked pretty much like I did before I was "saved." My words didn't change much. I stopped saying the "bad swear" words, but I never gave much thought to the slang, idle words I was saying.

Myself, I am an outgoing person. I never really need to be prompted to speak, I will carry on a conversation with someone that I don't know anything about. It isn't hard for me to be social.

But something has changed.

When we were visiting the Amish homes, I noticed something different about the women…..when talking with them, they were "slow to speak." It was almost as if they hesitated before they spoke to ensure that they would say the right thing. Not many joked around or even said "slang" words like I was using.

Why make the change:

When one becomes a Christian there is an expectancy that a change of speech follows because living for Christ makes a difference in one's choice of words.

But I say unto you, That every idle word that men shall speak, they shall give account thereof in the day of judgment.

Matthew 12:36

Seeing then that we have such hope, we use great plainness of speech:
Jesus reminds us that the words we speak are actually the overflow of our hearts

2 Corinthians 3:12

out of the abundance of the heart the mouth speaketh.

Matthew 12:34

I am writing this because it was brought to my attention by another Christian woman, in love. Do I think that it is a sin to say these words? That is something that you need to ask God about. These have just become my personal convictions for cleaning up my speech.

The following words are words that I have worked on/are working on eliminating from my speech:

"**Oh my**", "**oh my gosh**", or "**Oh my goodness**"—all of these words and various forms of it are just a substitute from the typical words "Oh my G-d" that people so haphazardly use.

"**Kid**", now this doesn't sound so bad but when it was brought to my attention, I think more about using this word so loosely. In the bible it talks about the end times when God will separate the sheep from the goats. What is a baby goat called? A kid. Referring to your children as baby goats puts them into a predestined situation—according to some. Call them children instead.

"**oh crap!**" that is just another substitute for the other pile of manure people say.

good lord, gosh, jeepers, lordy, holy cow, these are all just substitutes for using God's name in vain. And I always ask whenever I hear holy cow..when did your cow become holy??

"What the heck"–another substitute for a place opposite of heaven

This is a list of some of the more slang words that I know I hear more frequently in Christian circles:

- ***Crap***
- ***Freakin'***
- ***Darn it***
- ***Dang it***
- ***Friggin'***
- ***Screwed***
- ***Shoot!***
- ***Shucks***
- ***Sucks***

How to make the change:

Okay now that I have listed most all of the words that we may have used, it is time to evaluate your speech. In your prayer time, ask God if any of those that you speak you should refrain from. Then it is time to work on it.

I don't think it is good to find a replacement for your "slang" words. Just as I don't think an addict needs to replace one drug with a less addicting one, neither one helps the situation. You are just replacing one bad for another. I think that what you need to evaluate is what triggers your response.

If you find that every time something goes wrong and you use the words, "oh cr-p," then you need to consciously be aware to not say anything at that moment.

If when someone gives you unexpected news and you are tempted to say, "oh my goodness" change it with "wow, really?" "that is sad."

There is always something better to replace a negative word in your speech. As with everything, it takes time and effort. That is why we are doing this 52 weeks of change. You are to challenge yourself for a week and if your speech is something you want to continue on with then you will continue working with it. If not, then you move onward to another challenge, easy as that.

Chapter 15

The change: to go TV free for 1 week

Ouch!! Now before we get all crazy, remember this is only for 1 week. It isn't forever, just a temporary step back to see how much more time you COULD have in your week if you would just shut off the TV.

In our home we haven't had broadcast TV in a long time. But we do have many DVD's that we like to watch and I know that to occupy my children I like to put on a video for them to watch. Yes, I am guilty of using the TV as a babysitter more times than once.

One of my favorite things about visiting the Amish homes is that they don't own a television. It doesn't mean that they haven't watched it before, just that they choose not to have one in their homes. What a blessing I would come to learn.

Why make the change:

I know that I can personally evaluate my own life and look at how many hours are wasted sitting around in front of the television. Much disconnect happening within the family and no real communication going on.

If you were to ask any of my children how it was when we lost power for a week at our home, and they would ALL answer how great it was that we spent much time together talking and hanging out. Personally, I would like to be able to have my water and electricity still work but, I definitely enjoyed having the television shut off for that time. At first it was bothersome, I knew that I had to spend time reading to my children and not doing what "I" wanted to do. We spent more time talking and hanging out and bonding as a family.

When televisions are on, Dad comes home and he is tired from a long day at work so he sits in front of the TV. Children are excited because Dad is home and most of the time is spent telling them to "keep quiet" or "move" to get out of the way. Mom is tired from a long day with children and "plops down" to sit for hours in front of the TV. Not much family bonding going on. Imagine having nothing to turn to but our families instead of escaping to unreality?

As with everything it is difficult the first few times but after awhile it will be amazing at how much you talk and share things you normally don't talk about. You might even find things to do like play games, or re-connect with your spouse or child.

Some people may choose not to have a TV in the home because it is sometimes treated as an idol. I don't think I need to discuss the amount of inappropriate things seen on TV. I know you can control much with having your own DVD's but it still can open the door to things that are objectionable. It can start to become an addiction in your life something you MUST watch. How many shows are on that you just can't miss each week? How many inappropriate words are our children listening to because they are "allowed" on shows and movies?

How to make the change:

This one is easy, just shut it off. Yes, unplug it, move it if you have to, and do not turn it on for a week. Remember it is just for one week. It will be a little difficult especially when little ones start to cry and you just need to occupy them for 20 minutes, but try not to be tempted. Be prepared, include them in your work, promise a story when you are finished, make it enjoyable for them as well. At night time if you are inclined to watching TV, grab a book to read. Or better yet, catch up on much needed sleep. Your husbands' might even enjoy spending more time with you:)

Remember this is all about simplifying our life. If we can cut down on the chaos and wasted time we can be happier and more fulfilled in our days.

Chapter 16

The change: to exercise

Oops, probably not the one you wanted to hear, I know---- been there before. Always had an excuse, too busy, pregnant, just had a baby, no sleep, no time for anything. But……. I had time to feel miserable. I had time to lay in bed for hours because my back hurt. I had time to research why my body felt different, and time to go to the doctors for medication to fix things. But I couldn't find the time for preventative maintenance.

Why make the change:

When I was young, I felt great and could mainly eat whatever I wanted. I did not have to think about it affecting me. Well, then I got older. I had 10 babies and not much time in between to THINK about losing weight, it was all about survival. Then I grew tired. Tired of feeling tired, tired of feeling fat, tired of feeling miserable.

I needed a change. A long-term change. Yes, you can find every "miracle" cure to treat your ailments. "Eat pineapple for this, take this vitamin supplement for that." But none are going to get to the real issue. The real issue was that I was overweight. My body could not function properly because it was doing "overtime" work keeping my body going. I decided to change.

We all know or should know that we can't just expect our bodies to work properly if we don't exercise. Even if we think we are active enough, if we have "jiggle" on our body, more than likely we need to exercise. You can look at all the statistics on heart disease, arthritis, and find every ailment that starts to affect a person especially around 40 years of age. I am sure most of us knows someone that is taking numerous amount of medication because of health reasons. With some proper diet and exercise many of those pills could be gone.

We need to be doing preventative maintenance on ourselves. The time is minimal when compared to the shortening of our lifespan and the amount of time spent trying to control our health conditions. Did I mention the amount of money you will save by taking care of yourself now?

How to make the change:

I didn't change my eating habits at all in the beginning of my weight loss journey. But I did change the amount of activity that I did. I decided to exercise almost every day. I had babies and I had lots of little ones at that time. **5 under 5 to be exact!** But I chose to do it, I chose to exercise every day for myself. I started out by walking. I didn't go on long walks away from my children, I did it outside around my yard.

I did that for a few months and then my husband bought me an elliptical. My absolutely favorite thing! I would suggest looking for a used piece of equipment, as most people buy them in hopes of using them and then don't:) look on Craigslist for one in your area.

If you still aren't able to get outside or purchase equipment, be creative in your venture to exercise. I actually started dancing to my children's Wiggles videos and got a great workout for the half hour it was on. Try it, it was exhausting—those men are troopers:)

Get your children involved doing some of the following:

- sit ups
- push ups
- leg lifts
- squats
- march around the house, doing high knee lifts
- stretch—your arms, legs, back, and neck muscles

There are numerous FREE things you can do to exercise. If you really need help, look up some on YouTube or rent a video from the library–Denise Austin is my favorite.

Again, this is a challenge, try it for a week, but I would recommend three to see some results. See how you feel at the end of those weeks. Do you have more energy? Have you lost some weight? How about your mood? Does it make you want to continue? I pray it does. You will never regret exercising.

Chapter 17

The change: clear a counter

When you walk into your kitchen, what is the first thing that catches your eye? What are things that your husband sees as he is walking in the door after a long day at work? When you have guests, what do they see first?

I know that the counters can be a quick catch for everything that leads to clutter especially in a large family. But even if you have all the dishes done, the counters cleared of papers, and the food put away, our counters can still be cluttered with decorations and appliances that rarely get used.

Why make the change:

As with everything in life the more simplified we can make it, the more peaceful and calmer we will be. If we are constantly fumbling for something, or trying to find counter space for this item. If we have to move one mess just to make room for another mess. We are just adding chaos to our life.

How to make the change:

How do you go about de-cluttering and organizing your kitchen counters? First clean up your kitchen as you normally would, putting away all items that are not normally left out. Leave the room and walk back into the kitchen, pretending you are viewing it through the eyes of another person. What types of areas are your eyes drawn to? Is it the stack of papers and notes that you leave out because you need them every day? Or is it the many appliances that you leave out because you use them a few times per week? Is it the sink with its messy dish rag and bottle of soap? You need to identify areas that need de-cluttering and fix them.

Start with paperwork. You need to identify what the paperwork is and where it came from and then where it is supposed to go. Sort through your mail by the trash can and immediately throw away junk mail. Open the bills and place them in an area that you pay your bills at. Put the magazines and newspapers in the area that you read them at. After you have read the magazine or newspaper throw it away. If you have an article or recipe that you want to save from the publication then cut it out and place it in your household binder or in your recipe box. If it is paperwork for your husband, place it in an area just for that. If your counter-tops are covered in appliances, you need to reevaluate which ones you actually "need" out every day and which ones you can put away because it only takes seconds to get it out again.

Keep your counter-tops cleared. It is more pleasing to the eye and makes a nicer workplace for you to be in. Clearing the clutter from the kitchen is not a once and forever job, it is something that needs to be evaluated every few months. Clutter creeps up on us and we need to keep our eye on it so that it doesn't take over. Clutter makes our daily work harder to do because we have to fumble around it. You need to train yourself to constantly evaluate the clutter factor in the area where you are the most. For most of us ladies, it is the kitchen. Keep it clutter free. You just might be motivated to de-clutter other areas of "chaos" in your home.

Chapter 18

The change: to play more

This challenge might seem like one that you would just skip over, but I encourage you to view this with an open mind. I like the verse in 1 Corinthians 13:11

> *When I was a child, I spake as a child, I understood as a child, I thought as a child: but when I became a man, I put away childish things.*

I firmly believe that there are many "immature" adults out there that just need to learn to grow up. But I also firmly believe that there are many adults out there that need to "loosen up" a bit.

Where do you lie?

Why make the change:

This challenge came to me this week as I was invited to attend a ladies day away. Now I am not one to go out regularly. I firmly believe that I don't have to "get away" for my sanity. I should be able to find that in my home life. But I was invited and my daughter insisted she would watch the children. I even thought it might be fun to go with my good friends.

This event, which was a ladies night out at a church, was one of fun, let down your hair and just have a good time. We played some silly games, had fellowship, and all had a bunch of hearty good laughs.

Was that wrong? Was it wrong to go out and just have a time of relaxation and laughs?

No, I don't believe it was. I took care of my duties at home, made sure that my children were properly taken care of, that my husband approved, and then I went.

Would I do it every weekend? No......Once a month? Maybe......Once every few months? Most definitely.

How to make the change:

Is this easy for everyone? No probably not, especially if you are a mother of many little ones. I will admit that I had NEVER gotten away by myself in the last 8 years of having babies. I know might be sad, but I was either pregnant or nursing a baby and there wasn't time to go out. My free time was spent going to bed early to catch up on sleep.

But now, just in the past couple of years has been the first time that my husband and I have gone out to dinner ALONE, I have gotten to take my children out on Mom and child date nights, and I have been able to attend a few things by myself. But this is all a first.   It is just a new chapter in my life.

What about for the mom who has many little ones that cannot get away? I encourage you to make this change and do what it says-- PLAY with your children. Don't just change diapers, clean up, wipe them up, and get dinner ready. Take the time to get on the floor and play with them one on one. Take the time to get out the blocks and make a tower, while they knock it over again and again.

Just get down on their level and take the time out of your day and sit and enjoy playing with them. If you can get out, take them to the park and go down the slides with them, run around and chase them. Play games. Don't just sit on the bench and look at your phone. Engage and interact with your children.

You will be refreshed, as well as your child enjoying some fun time with you.

Take the time to either find some "play" time with your children, or see if there is an event at your local church for a Mom's night out. Grab a girlfriend and have a great time of fellowship.   It is good to be able to refresh your soul with a much needed break from the demands of being a wife and mother.

Chapter 19

The change: to live paper and plastic free

I love being informed as a consumer and as a parent. My husband and I quite often watch documentaries. We love to think outside of what our government and society is programming us to believe. Much of what we are led to believe is untrue. We as consumers need to start looking at things instead of just taking them as fact.

I just finished watching a documentary on plastic called "Bag It" by Reel Thing Film. Great video, I learned some things that I didn't already know about plastic and things I should think more about that I don't already.

Why make the change:

Plastic is made from fossil fuels, which is a non-renewable source. Once they are gone there isn't any more of it.

In the United States we go through 1 million plastic bags per minute according to the film.

Disposables. Why are we making something like say a disposable coffee cup, that we are going to use for maybe 20 minutes and then throw it away? Especially when that item was made from a non-renewable source, and it took thousands of years to make. Plus if that coffee cup was made with Styrofoam it is going to be around forever.

300 million disposable coffee cups per day are used.

1 million plastic cups used on airplane flights in 6 hours.

60,000 plastic bags consumed in the US every 5 seconds.

There is more plastic produced from 2000-2010 then the entire 1900's.

Most all of the plastic eventually goes from landfills and gets into our water system which ultimately ends up in our oceans.

Do a Google search on **North Pacific gyre**. It is one of many huge garbage patches out in the middle of the ocean. It isn't so much big chunks of plastic that can be cleaned up, it is plastic that has been broken down into smaller chunks and it is just floating in masses out in the water.

There are many beaches that are just covered in tiny bits of plastic from all of the garbage that gets washed ashore. Hawaii is one of them. Do some searching on your own, it is there just not readily available.

The damage it is doing to our wildlife is dangerous as well. Most of the dead animals that they do autopsies on having numerous plastic items inside their stomachs. It would be like us having our bowl of cereal for breakfast plus a handful of Styrofoam peanuts. Yuck!

There are many dangers to plastic as well. BPA and phylates have been in the media lately and thankfully some have been removed from items. But not completely. Chemical use in products in America is innocent until proven guilty that they are dangerous to humans. In other countries it is the opposite, they have the consumers interest in mind verses their paychecks.

All information taken from the documentary "Bag It" from Reel Thing Films

How to make the change:

What can we do as consumers?

- Cut back on single item purchases, like snack sized items.
- Don't drink bottled water.

- Buy things with less packaging.
- Buy things used.
- Bring your own containers.
- Buy less stuff.
- Simplify your life.

Sometimes the best things to do are to rethink the way you do things. Our grandparents never had plastics and they did just fine in life. We just need to get creative in the way that we do things. Think plain and simplify.

Try and go all week without using a disposable plastic or paper product. If you are going to be reusing them like a plastic bag that you will wash out, then that is okay. But try and not use any that will be put in the trash for waste. It will be hard. But a little bit of cutting back is much better than none at all.

Chapter 20

The change: choosing to be happy

Just sitting here pondering why would people not choose to be happy? It is a question that baffles me frequently. I know many people that are just generally unhappy. They feel distressed with the worries of life, joyless in their daily interactions, and just feel like they got stuck with the "short end of the stick." Why would someone choose that wretched path of life?

If you were to ask someone what they most want out of life, I would suspect that majority of people would give answers like, "to be successful," "to make a lot of money," and "**to be happy**." Why when given the notion they choose unhappiness?? By being happy, you can make more money, find a better job and be better motivated to reach those goals that will make you successful in your life.

Why make the change:

Why aren't people happy?? If you look around there are loads of books about happiness, the sermons at church are about feeling good and being happy, and many magazine articles about the art of happiness. Even in our US Constitution it says "Life, Liberty, and the pursuit of Happiness." Why is it hard to make that decision to be happy?

At about the time you hit the teenage age, your brain starts losing part of its chemical makeup that helps us be happy, it is called dopamine. Dopamine is what our brain makes when it is happy. Depending upon circumstances and how you choose to react to situations, your brain either makes dopamine, or the cells slowly start to die off. If you don't use them by being happy, they will slowly start to wither away. Research has shown that the cells do not regenerate. It is a use it or lose it situation.**

One way to help use the cells and make dopamine is through physical activity. Being on the move, exercising, doing things out of the "norm" to stimulate our brains in a positive way, are all good things to help dopamine growth.

People believe that if good things happen you will be happier, or if you have bad things happen your life will be bad forever. But the reality is when you go through bad things, people generally bounce back and do move on with their life in happiness. Sometimes a bad thing needs to happen in order for us to learn from it and put things in perspective in our lives.

What made us happy before internet, television, cars, etc? Go back 80 years or go to remote village tribes who are void to all of our modernized world and their happiness is based on **community**. Belonging to a "family," helping each other out, being responsible for others in every aspect of their lives is what made and still makes people genuinely happier.

Compassion and love for one another is a lost art in our society. Most of us, don't even know our own neighbors.

**taken from the documentary Happy by Wadi Rum Films, Inc.

How to make the change:

What is the most effective in achieving happiness in life?

Having gratitude, counting your blessings, and acts of kindness. These are all great ways to achieving happiness. Things that help you look at something bigger than yourself. If you only seek your own happiness in life it is kind of selfish. But once you worry about the well-being of the world, your life grows. You care about something bigger than yourself.

If each of us spent a smidgen of time each day practicing happiness or other virtuous qualities like compassion etc, our world would really be a better place. We should be looking at happiness as a skill. Just as we would want to learn to play piano, or to cook, we should really want to learn to be happier.

The formula for happiness is not the same for everyone. But the things we do are the building blocks of our life. Play, having new experiences, friends and family, doing things that are meaningful, and appreciating what we have, these are what makes us happy and they are free. And with happiness the more we have the more everyone has.

Chapter 21

The change: to be thankful

I believe we should all be thankful each and every day of our lives not just at Thanksgiving time. We should be daily thanking our Savior for all that we do have.

But what if you say Amy, I can't really think of much I am thankful for this year. Maybe it was a bad year, maybe you lost a loved one, maybe you are just in a deep depressive state and can't think of anything to be thankful for, or maybe you are in a state of self pity. Whatever the reasons, you need to remember these words:

"in everything give thanks; for this is the will of God in Christ Jesus for you."

1 Thessalonians 5:18

That verse means that we give thanks in the good times and in the bad times. It is really easy to give God the glory and praise when things are going good. It's great to say, "Look what the Lord has done." But try saying that when you are going through a big struggle in your life. Maybe it's a relationship problem, maybe its personal addictions, maybe it is something even you or I cannot fathom. What about those times? In the midst of troubled times we need to still give God the glory.

Why make the change:

What is something we gain from going through hard times??

STRENGTH

When Job was tested by the devil, he remained faithful and steadfast always thanking God. In the end, Job was doubly rewarded. In the same way, we, too, will grow stronger, and receive a great reward from God if we hold true to Him, and are thankful for the hard times.

One of the greatest rewards is being identified with Jesus Christ, and when we suffer, all the while being thankful, we are taking Christ's attitude, and people will see it! Later, we will be able to help others because of the strength that God gave us because of the hard struggles.

Isn't that true? Isn't it great to come across another mother who has gone through the same struggles as you are currently going through? Or maybe you can come across a blog that fits your circumstances in your life. There are blogs for everything, we are encouraging one another on a HUGE level. I am thankful for the technology that we do have to be able to share and to be encouraged by other woman.

How to make the change:

When times are tough, start stating things you are thankful for. There is ALWAYS something we can be thankful for. It is a choice, one that will decide what type of day you will have, what type of person you will become, and what type of influence you will make on the world.

Chapter 22

The change: To write a letter

This might sound simple because you think that it will "qualify" since you write emails and text friends with encouraging notes almost every day. But I am talking about getting out that stationary—yes they do make it—and sit down and write an old fashioned letter to a friend.

Why make the change:

Why, do you ask, would I encourage you to write a letter to someone? I don't think anyone can disagree with me that it is exciting to be able to receive something in the mail, especially when it is just for them. What a blessing it is, especially for "us" moms, who are home each and every day to walk out to our mailboxes, expecting to receive advertisements and bills and then come upon a letter addressed to us.

It is a refreshing lift to our spirits to think that someone took the time to write a note of encouragement. I know for myself, it is one of the brightest joys to my day. Especially when the days were tough and I didn't get to look at emails or even answer a phone call during the day. But it was a joy to receive a letter in the mail, something I could sit down to, when it was convenient, and enjoy a moment of encouragement from a friend.

How to make the change:

How do we go about writing a letter? For starters you want to have some nice stationary. I know for myself, I used to write on plain notebook paper. Yes it was all I had and I didn't really have the time to look for nicer paper at the store so it was my excuse, but now I know where the stationary is in my local store so it is no excuse to be sending out notebook paper notes:) It is very inexpensive, you can even pick up a packet of blank note cards for writing shorter notes.

In your letters you want to start out with some encouraging news. I would use the default of "God" and start it out with an inspiring verse. Maybe one that you have been thinking about that week. Write a short line about the verse and how it is working in your life.

The rest of your letter should remain positive. Don't drag your friend down with news that is despairing. Don't dwell on the negatives in your life. Speak about the positives. I like to go through and give some tidbits of what each of my children are up to. I like to put some things that I am working on, some things that I am going to be working on in my own personal life, and ask for some prayer in those areas if needed.

I like to include a favorite recipe that we have enjoyed as a family. I write it out on index cards—yes you should do it on nicer recipe cards–but until I find those....index cards will have to do:)

Sometimes I like to add a packet of tea that I enjoy drinking. You can put in a packet of seeds, a prayer card, anything small and unexpected.

If you don't have the time to write a lengthy letter, write short encouraging letters to friends that you know might be going through a hard time. Give them some verses of encouragement and let them know you are praying for them.

I know for myself personally, this is something that can easily get forgotten in my life. I have just recently marked it on my calendar twice a month on my office days to write a letter to a friend. I know what a blessing it is and how much WE need to have encouragement from our friends something besides the internet or our own Bibles. We need tangible evidence from friends to know that the Lord is working through people to encourage and love us through all of our tough times.

Think of someone whom you can send a letter to this week, and I challenge that you continue on with this practice for life.

Chapter 23

The change: to take a daily vitamin.

Taking a daily vitamin has become a way of life for myself. I have been pregnant and nursing babies for most of my marriage. I have ALWAYS been on a prenatal vitamin and when I went off of it, I noticed that my hair and nails didn't grow as well. I have been sure to get back on the track of taking one daily, even though I am not currently nursing or am not pregnant. Prevention is a good thing.

With my children, my first set of four, I never really pushed giving them a vitamin each day. My second set of six, I am sure to give them one every day and I can honestly say that I believe it helps in preventing colds and sickness. We still get sickness but not as much as we did in the past. Plus the children's overall health has been better. I would definitely recommend making sure your child takes one. We take the one with "Plus extra C".

Why make the change:

Vitamins should not be viewed as the "cure all" for our American life. Most people instead of eating healthy and exercising will think that by taking a vitamin will ensure that they won't get certain diseases or will assume that it will erase all of their bad eating. But it does not. A multi vitamin is a "fill in" per se for nutrients that you might not receive on a daily basis.

I know to be responsible to provide nutrients to a nursing or in the womb child, I made sure to take one every day. Then if I was lacking, I would be covered.

Now that I am losing weight, I know that my diet is not full of every vitamin that I need on a daily basis. Taking a vitamin supplement ensures that my body will not be devoid of those vitamins while I am temporarily cutting back on certain foods in order to lose a few pounds.

Even if my diet returns to the normal whole foods healthy choices, I will probably receive all of the vitamins and minerals that my body will need. But as a Mom who could conceive at any time, I like to take the vitamin to ensure that my body is properly protected in case I would be carrying a life inside of me and not know it, while all of the important organs were forming:) better to be safe than sorry.

How to make the change:

Purchase a multi vitamin and take one each day. I like to take mine in the evening, as to avoid stomach upset. Drink with water.

I know that our society is filled with the vitamin supplement craze right now and there are supplements for everything. Instead of taking an "extra" vitamin, I would suggest looking into whole foods that are "rich" in that vitamin and be sure to eat more of that each day.

It is ALWAYS better to receive our nutrition from food than a pill. Taking a multi vitamin is just a way to fill in the gaps if we are lapse during our days. Is isn't a cure all, but something that will aid us in taking care of our bodies properly.

Chapter 24

The change: to gather up your fragments

To gather up your fragments means to use what you have without having to search elsewhere for supplies. This week, I want you to avoid shopping. Yes, I said that correctly AVOID grocery shopping. I hope that you have a small stash of groceries left in your pantry and a few pieces of meat or beans in your freezer. Maybe you have looked around in your pantry and thought it would be easier just to go shopping this week so that you don't have to "think" about making dinner. Even though there is still plenty of food in the pantry.

Why make the change:

Most of us over spend on everything, ME included. I will go shopping just because I do the same thing once a month and it is time to do that. I don't always wait, even though I could. But there were times when I was unable to do shopping due to an unexpected financial emergency. We had to do without and guess what? We didn't starve and no one went to bed hungry either.

I was just creative and "gathered up my fragments and used what I had." It was times like that, that I realized that we ate too many wasteful foods. I noticed that my children got fuller on staple foods like rice and beans. I realized that without cookies and sugar filled snacks they were actually acting better. I also realized that I could purchase food inexpensively and feed my children a better diet when I wasn't buying all of the extras like chips, pop, and ice cream.

Some of our favorite meals are "surprise dinners." When I handed my children their dinner plate I said "surprise!" and they ate it and loved it:) It was a mixture of items that we had on hand. But it made a great dish. Sometimes my husband will ask, "Can you make this again?" I laugh because it is usually a dish that I threw a bunch of ingredients together in.

How to make the change:

Well this part will be hard. How can I tell you how to throw a bunch of ingredients together and make something? I recommend that you think casserole or soup type meal depending upon what you have. For myself we make many casseroles. I normally always have rice on hand. I can throw some beans, diced tomatoes, spices and then put it over top of rice for my famous surprise chili. It usually contains a bit of leftover salsa, alfredo sauce, and taco seasoning.

The key is to use what you have. Be creative and think what sort of things might taste good together. I discovered that chicken tenderloins cooked in 1000 island dressing tastes really good. We served it over noodles coated with a butter and garlic mixture.

We also have many eggs, but sometimes we don't always have the breakfast meats to put into it. My daughter used pepperoni cut up and guess what? Everyone thought it was the best tasting eggs ever!

Making haystacks are a filling meal and easy to make. We use the following foods and then layer them. Use whatever ingredients you have or add some of your own.

- cooked rice
- refried beans
- black beans
- corn
- shredded lettuce
- shredded cheese
- salsa
- green onions
- sour cream or ranch

Your task this week is to dig into that pantry and look deep into that freezer. Be creative and see if you can go all week without shopping. Put that extra money NOT SPENT into a special envelope marked vacation or savings. See how much you can accumulate by gathering up your fragments once a month.

Chapter 25

The change: to pray

For many of us, we pray. We might only pray when things go wrong or when we need something and that is not the kind of prayer that I am encouraging. Even though those things are good to pray for, this week's challenge is to encourage you to pray MORE. Pray more to thank God for His blessings. Pray more for someone other than yourself. Pray more for the healing of our country. Pray for God to restore a marriage, a broken friendship, a broken relationship. Prayer for someone other than ourselves.

Why make the change:

Why should we pray for someone other than ourselves? It is good to think of others. Sometimes when we start taking the focus off of what "our needs" are, we are better equipped to help serve and encourage others who might be needing some love.

It is easy to sit around and dwell about all the bad things that we need fixing in our own life. I know I could sit and talk with the Lord and ask him for wisdom to guide me and to help fix this and fix that, but what I should be focusing on is thanking HIM for what He does each and every day.

My days should be continually praising Him for the sun, or the clouds, or the majestic earth we are part of. The beauty in my children, the joys of my life, and praising Him for saving my wretched soul, when I wasn't deserving. Thanking Him in all of my bad situations and problems in my life. I know that God will turn good out of all those negative things in my life.

When I pray for someone else, God can use that to show me something that I could do for that person. Maybe he will show me how I can physically do something for them, or He can give me words to speak to that person. When we are open to listening to God and seeking His counsel in prayer He will speak to us and give us words to give to others.

How to make the change:

How do we pray more? Have a plan. For myself, I could easily go through my whole day and forget to pray, I know not very Christian of me. But I am human and busy with lots of little ones. I need to make it a point to pray. I need to specifically set aside a time of my day when I can pray and thank God for things.

When I had lots of little ones, my only time was when I was in the shower. I know many people might think that is unacceptable and that I should of gotten up before my babies and had alone time with the Lord. But I know the Lord knows my heart and the shower was my prayer time. As I went about my day, I would take the time when I was washing the dishes and looking out the window to remind myself to pray and thank God for things. It wasn't a formal prayer of bowing my head, but I can easily speak to HIM while washing dishes. While I was rocking my babies and nursing them to sleep, I might sing praise songs while thinking of the Lord.

Sometimes prayer doesn't have to be going inside a closet, shutting the door for 30 minutes, and bowing your head and closing your eyes. Sometimes it can be while taking a shower, while washing dishes, or while holding a baby. God knows where you are at and He knows your heart. He just wants you to acknowledge Him, to take time to thank Him.

I encourage you to keep praying and praising Him even when life gets busy. If you can't take the time because you are physically exhausted and have no help then my prayer is for you today:

Lord, I thank you for opportunities and the time to write this book. I pray that you continue to use this to encourage others.
My prayer for today is that you will give Mothers the time to spend with you. Give them time where their children will sleep a little bit longer, or you will occupy the little ones so that Mom can sit and have a moment alone with you. I know Lord how hard it

was to find that time to seek you, but I thank you for praying women who helped remind me of the times that I could find alone with you. My prayer is that women will know how important it is to stay focused on YOU and not get burdened down with the large amount of responsibilities and tasks that it takes to run a household and raise up children. My prayer is that they will focus on YOU and that you will give them peace and wisdom as they raise their children for you. Give them strength and unity among their families so that we raise up a Godly army for YOU.

In your name I pray and if you believe this say AMEN!!!—which means I say this in agreement.

Chapter 26

The change: to clean a closet

How many of you, when you open your closet, look at its contents, and think, "I don't have anything to wear today?" That is something many woman see while looking into their closets. Even though there is a mass of clothing, an unlimited number of shoes and purses, we as women can still look at it and think that we need more. Off we then go and purchase more unnecessary items to help fill our emotional need for MORE.

Why make the change:

The reason for this challenge is to help you simplify your life. Simplify means to get rid of, do without, do with less, and declutter. We want to be able to open up our closets and see a uniformed layout of choices. You should have from 7-10 choices. It shouldn't take long, or much thought to sift through your clothing choices. Clothing choices shouldn't overwhelm you. You want to make life simpler and it begins when you wake up in the morning and choose what to wear for the day.

How to make the change:

Here is the hard part. Most everyone has emotional ties to everything that they have. That is why we live the life full of STUFF. This stuff is starting to overtake us, overwhelm us and we need to make it STOP. It begins with one closet. This method will take over a few days to do.

To begin, sort ALL your clothing into 3 piles.

1. The ones you want to keep.
2. The ones you want to donate to others.
3. The ones that are maybe.

Remember all clothing that is worn, ripped, or seen its last days, has to go immediately into the TRASH pile.

Then you are going to go through your keep pile. You are going to check for any repairs that need to be done, make sure that they all fit you, and then start to organize them.

Organizing will be different for everyone, here is the method that I use. Begin to sort them into different piles. Piles for:

- skirts–everyday, and dressy
- t-shirts to wear under tops
- long t-shirts to wear under tops
- short sleeved tops
- long sleeved tops
- summer sleeveless tops
- dresses
- sweaters/overcoats

Within my grouping of skirts for example, I will see how many long skirts I have. I really only need 3-4 skirts. I keep two nicer skirts for dressing up. Plus a few lighter ones for warmer weather.

For my t-shirts to wear under tops, I keep it simple, I buy all brown. I have learned over the years to cater my wardrobe a certain color scheme, to keep it simple. I make it easy and keep four brown t-shirts to fit under my regular tops for modesty. It is much easier to just grab a brown undershirt and know it goes with one of my tops.

Since my life consists of children and working at home, I don't have the need for many dressy outfits. I keep my clothing neat and clean, somewhat dressed up, but also easy to be able to do hundreds of dishes a day in.

I have a few dressier clothing for special occasions and church. I keep one sweater for warmth.

My shoes are simple. I have a brown pair of leather boots and dress shoes. One pair of running shoes and one pair of hiking shoes (A necessity since moving to the mountains.) I also keep a few pairs of sandals and flip flops for warmer weather.

Next you are going to go through your maybe pile. After you have gone through your keep pile, you know how many outfits that you own, keep that in mind when deciding what to do with your maybe pile. Ask yourself, "Do you really need to keep an outfit that maybe you will wear one day?" Get rid of the "one day" mentality. That day may never come. Stop buying things because they look cute. Think necessity not availability.

Gather up your donations and take them to a women and children's shelter. Check your local churches for donations.

You might have to do this a few times over the next month. If you keep staring at it in your closet and you are not wearing it within the month, get rid of it. With exceptions to special occasion outings. Enjoy looking at your "lean" closet with order and purpose.

Chapter 27

The change: To eat popcorn for a snack

This might sound like a challenge that doesn't quite fit into the 52 weeks less stuff more life challenge, but in essence it does. How many times a week do you grab those chips, cookies, or other snacky foods to fulfill your cravings? What I want you to do this week is swap out your favorite snacks in exchange for air popped popcorn.

Why make the change:

For some of us, we eat poorly. We eat processed foods because they taste great. We are overweight. We are bound to snack companies for their foods that make us fat, clog our arteries, and are turning our children into diabetic adults. We need to stop this madness. It all begins with a bowl of air popped popcorn. Sounds simple right?

Did you know that popcorn seeds are very inexpensive? They cost a fraction of the price of a bag of chips or bag of candy.

Did you know that you can get the benefits of eating whole grains with popcorn? Popcorn contains fiber which is a necessary dietary need. Many of us do not receive enough in our daily diet.

Did you know that popcorn is a dieters dream come true? Popcorn is a great "filler" food that when properly made, can contain only a trace amount of calories per serving. Which in turn means that you can eat a huge abundance of it and not gain many calories from it.

How to make the change

In our family it begins with a 25 pound bag of popcorn seeds. We keep this in a five gallon bucket in our pantry. We fill up our air popcorn popper and start popping. We fill our largest bowl.

After the bowl is filled, we spray it lightly with spray butter and sprinkle sea salt on it.

For those that would like more of a flavoring but still stay healthier than a bag of chips, I would recommend getting popcorn flavorings. We enjoy the white cheddar and ranch flavors. They are a much better alternative than oil laden potato chips but still give your popcorn a nice flavor. We have also done melted chocolate drizzled over top, if we are looking for a "sweet" treat. Nice for people looking to cut back on deserts. You still get a bit of chocolate taste, but you eat more plain popcorn to fill you up.

Try this for a week, see how much better you feel by substituting this for snack foods. Continue doing it for the next few weeks and see the difference in weight loss.

Chapter 28

The change: to praise your spouse and/or children:

You might think this one is easy to do, but I know for myself it is something that can easily become forgotten during my days.

Our days are filled with a whirlwind of things that just keep coming and going and moving and changing and it makes our days filled with busyness. If I don't purposefully make a point to praise my husband and child, then most of the time, I just get busy and don't say it.

Why make the change:

This answer to the question is very easy….."Because we ALL crave praise." Each and every one of us, enjoys getting praise from someone. It should come from the people that are the closest to us, our spouses, parents, and children.

Praise a child and they will have a happier attitude, a better outlook on their day, and you can usually get a better work repertoire out of them. But forget to say encouraging praising words to them and suddenly their days are filled with drudgery jobs and parents that bark orders.

Same is true for our spouses. We both go to work just in different environments. If we forget to say positive words of praise to each other, then when days get hard and long, it is much easier to look at things and become bitter towards the other individual. But have a smiling happy spouse say to you, "Wow, you are doing a great job, even though that is really tough," and life suddenly gets more bearable.

How to make the change:

This week, focus on speaking positive words to your spouse and your children. Think when the words that come out of our mouths, will go into our own ears as well as other people's, and then they will drop down into our souls. Once there, they will give us either joy or sadness. We want to be people who speak joy and happiness into other's lives.

Set your calendar reminder on your phone to go off at different intervals throughout the day. When it does, send a positive praising text to your husband.

When working with your child, over emphasize what they are doing by praising them. Do it "too much" so that they know that you really do care. Once you have a realization of doing it "too much" you will be able to notice more when it needs to be said. It will become more of a habit and routine thus easily remembered.

Chapter 29

The change: to let go of guilt

One of the hardest lessons in life is letting go. Whether it's guilt, anger, love, loss, etc. Change is never easy, you fight to hold on, and you fight to let go.

author unknown

Do you ever wish you could change your past? Do things of the past affect your daily living in the areas of:

- eating-by how much or how little you eat
- the way you treat your spouse
- the way you treat your children
- how hard it is to say "no"
- how you spend your money on unnecessary items
- how you spend your quite time, dwelling over the "what if's" or the "could-of, should-of, would-of" lines."

Guilt is often a self-created reminder of all the things we wish we had done differently for ourselves. No one wants to be reminded of being the cause of someone else's pain, or that something they did caused a major problem. Most everyone has lived with guilt, letting it bother them in every decision they have made in life. Guilt comes from regret, which comes from fear. Living in fear is something God does not want us to do.

Deuteronomy 31:6 says:
"Be strong and courageous. Do not be afraid or terrified because of them, for the LORD your God goes with you; he will never leave you nor forsake you."

Most of us will just push that lesson aside and let it fester like a sore, and it will continue festering for life. It affects us as we go about our daily ways, physically, emotionally, and socially.

Why make the change:

We all need reminders. We need to know that we are not our mistakes or mishaps. We all do things for which we feel bad about in hindsight. We question our thought or actions, we wish to turn back the hands of time and do differently. Sometimes it is not possible to clean up our mess easily. Yet, we feel as if we should suffer.

We continue to allow the guilt to eat us from the inside out. This in turn forces us to stay stationary in a thought, which prevents us from healing, moving forward, owning our mess, and seeing what can be done.

This is NOT a healthy way to live. This will not benefit you or others around you. We want to live life to the fullest and know that things happen and there isn't a whole lot we can do about them. We can just accept, get over, and keep pressing forward.

How to make the change:

This might sound easier than it is said. I can tell you from personal experience, it is well worth it to work through it. You will never be able to fully live out your life in a positive manner if you live in bondage of guilt.

It takes more courage and more strength to get up even when we feel wounded. I encourage you to make the strides, even if you still feel devastated. You cannot remain in tragic limbo hurting. A period of a time for mourning the person we wish we had been, is normal and expected. Even though the person we can become awaits, as we punish ourselves for actions we can no longer retrieve.

We can make a change. Decide to get up, make a plan, encourage ourselves to address what we did, and find a way to work on it.

Here are some practical ways to address guilt:

1. Write it down. Use a journal and write a letter to God about all of the guilt you are expressing. Keep it and you can review it later. You may be surprised at how you feel a few days later.
2. Entrust in a good friend. Sometimes sharing and talking with a close friend will help you sort through your feelings of guilt. Sometimes what you thought was a big deal was not really a big deal at all.
3. Forgive and move onward. Obsessing over what you could have done in the past keeps you from focusing on the present. Address your guilt and make amends with whomever you feel you've wronged. Realize that things just happen and there isn't much that we can do to prevent them.
4. When guilt starts to creep up on you for not doing something, or for something you may have done wrong– immediately start rebuking that thought. Start focusing on the positive side of things not the negative.
5. If you feel that you need to apologize to someone, then do it. You need to go with a humbled attitude. Expect that the other person may not receive it, and that is okay. State your peace, don't get into arguments, and leave it.

Your past CANNOT determine your future. It can be wiped clean and started over fresh. Don't let your struggle become your identity.

Chapter 30

The change: to bake a treat this week

There is something that each of us may remember about walking into Grandma's kitchen and smelling her delicious homemade sugar cookies or freshly baked pie in the oven. Whatever your memories may be, get back to them. Embrace them and let your children, grandchildren, or just yourself enjoy some good homemade treats.

Why make the change:

How simple it is to go to the local grocery store and purchase a package of chocolate chip cookies? We can even go to our local coffee shop and grab a whole tray of conveniently made treats. But what about the simplicity in making some yourself? Besides the fact that they are much healthier for you then store bought ones, the taste can't compare to fresh, warm treats out of the oven.

This challenge is all about simplifying your life and that includes your diet. Take a look on the back of the package of baked treats. Most of the ingredients are hard to pronounce and they are entering your body and doing damage to your insides. You can easily make the same treat with about less than ten ingredients. Plus, you know what you put into the treats and you can feel good knowing that your children are eating something that was prepared by you.

How to make the change:

We need to be teaching and training our children or grandchildren the fine art of baking. Is it too hard? No, baking is something each of us can do with a little practice.

Choose something simple. Look at the ingredients, if it has many things and lots of steps to the recipe, then skip it and go on to something else. Keep it simple until you are comfortable baking items.

Replace your store bought treats with one baked item this week. Hopefully you will enjoy it much more and will continue doing this for the rest of the year.

Chapter 31

The change: to bless others

Give, and it shall be given unto you; good measure, pressed down, and shaken together, and running over, shall men give into your bosom. For with the same measure that you give it shall be measured to you again.

Luke 6:38

Would you agree that by looking at your own life you would consider most things a blessing when compared to how the rest of the world lives? If you live in the United States, I am sure you would agree because it is obvious that we have been given freedom that many people do not have.

We have been given opportunities that many people don't have. We've been given material, physical, and spiritual abundance that a lot of people around the world simply do not have. Because of all of this, we MUST consider ourselves blessed.

Why make the change:

For unto whomsoever much is given, of him shall be much required: and to whom men have committed much, of him they will ask the more.

Luke 12:48

It is clear in God's word that to whom much is given, much is expected. In His word it says that we should use our blessings to bless others. In turn, when we bless others, God takes care of our needs.

The more you try to bless other people in the world around you, the more God says, *"I'm going to pour my blessings out on you."* It is almost like He will play a little game. Let's see who will win. Let's see who can give the most. The more you bless others the more I'm going to bless you in return.

How to make the change:

What are some ways you can bless others? There are numerous things you can do, here are a few:

1. Make a meal for a family. Maybe someone you know could use some extra help at dinner time–a new mom, a sick family member, maybe a single person who would enjoy someone else cooking for the night.
2. How about a cold or hot drink to the service worker who is outside all day. Your mail person, garbage man, or maybe lawn maintenance. I am sure on a freezing cold day, they would enjoy a hot cup of coffee.
3. Every pay for the person behind you in a fast food drive thru? Try it, it could catch on.
4. Pray for someone. Talking to God to help remove burdens can be a huge blessing. Pray, and start seeing things happen.
5. Write a letter of appreciation to someone. A heartfelt thank you letter for all that someone does, will brighten their day.
6. Volunteer. Check out your local soup kitchen, hospital, or elderly care facility. I am sure they would enjoy a new face to visit with.
7. Financially bless. Know someone who could use a financial blessing? Try this, BE BOLD and do it in secret so that your left hand does not know what your right hand is doing:)
8. Send a text filled with motivation and scripture to someone for the day.
9. Go through your home and donate items that you have no need for.
10. Surprise a friend or co worker with a birthday celebration. Investigate when their birthday is and surprise with a special lunch and dessert.

The best way to know who, or what, or how to bless is to ask God. Ask Him what it is you can do to help others. He promises to bless those that are a blessing. Try it see how wonderful He is and how it will come back to you.

Chapter 32

The change: to get rid of paper clutter

If you want to live a plainer lifestyle it is going to involve cutting back on things. One area that can get overwhelming is the paper clutter. Between the junk mail, magazine subscriptions, little notes scribbled to remind you to do something, and paper work from your child's school, your house can become an overwhelming whirlwind of paper. It doesn't have to be this way.

Why make the change:

Decluttering is a skill that you will learn with more practice just like any skill. In time you will be able to completely clear off a counter top filled with paper without even hesitating on what to do with each paper. It will become almost a normal instinct. In turn this will make your life smoother, and less stressful as you will not always view things drowning in paperwork.

How to make the change:

You are going to start with your pile of papers.

Toss any magazines, in reality you are not going to do anything with them. If you really wanted to save something, as you are reading it, rip out the recipe, or information and put it where it is needed.

Go through all mail. Quickly decide if it is junk mail, if it is then pitch it. If it is a bill, pay it immediately. Maybe something that requires your action—set in a folder specifically used for that.

Here are some tips to reduce paper clutter in your home:

- Look for ways to reduce your paper clutter. You can sign up online to stop receiving junk mail in your mailbox.
- Toss any junk mail immediately when receiving it.

- Sign up for electronic bill paying—no paperwork in the mail.
- Keep a filing cabinet for all necessary receipts and important paperwork that must be kept. Go through this once a year and weed out items that you no longer need.
- Scan items and get rid of your paper trail.
- Take photos of your child's school and art work. You can make them a digital book when they get older.

You should set aside a day each week that you take care of all your paperwork. If you are overwhelmingly taken by paper, then do this once a day until it is gone. If you are caught up then do this once a week. Whenever paper comes into the house, immediately decide what to do with it. Get rid of it, file immediately, or take action.

Chapter 33

The change: to clear your inbox

When we think of decluttering or simplifying we are to think about subtracting things out of our lives. To some this is hard, they want to hold onto every moment and every memory. It is something that needs to be changed. We need to do our best to declutter our lives. A life full of "stuff" is a life of constant managing, organizing, moving around and work. A life of "simplicity" is a life full of peace, contentment, and just time to say "ahhhhhhh."

One of these changes includes the area you probably frequent at least once per day—your email inbox.

Why make the change:

Our world has turned to online media and most all of us has an email. Our email box can get just as overloaded with saved emails, or emails waiting to be responded to, as our closets can with too many clothes.

This challenge is about simplifying every area of our life and this is one of the area's that can become overwhelming.

How to make the change:

Here are some simple steps to achieving a simplified inbox:

1. Don't check your email first thing in the morning. When you sit down first thing in the morning and go through emails you get stuck going through tons of emails. Do other tasks first and leave your email to be done later on. Designate a set time and stick with it.
2. When you check your email do something with it right away. Decide what needs to be done and do it.
3. If it is junk or forwarded mail, trash it immediately.

4. If it is a long email, print it off to be read at a later date, or file it to be read at a later time while having lunch or waiting in a doctor's office.
5. If the email requires a task, make a note on a list of what needs to be done and file your email in your archive. That way you can access it at a later date.
6. If you can do a quick response, do so immediately and then get rid of it.
7. If you need to save the email while you are waiting for a response, create a folder for that purpose.

In any case, emptying your email's inbox will leave you with a satisfaction of completing something simple and easy.

Chapter 34

The change: to plan a week of simple dinners.

Around the dinner hour, do you find yourself stressed because you are scampering around the kitchen trying to quickly thaw the meat, cook the noodles, and chop the vegetables? Let me guess, you didn't plan and prepare for dinner? When your husband walks in the door, you have to say, "Sorry honey, I wasn't able to get dinner made today, it was WAY too busy of a day." Is that the truth? or is it that you just didn't plan ahead? By simply planning a menu and preparing some simple tasks, you can have a dinner on your table every night, ON TIME!

Why make the change:

If figuring out what you are going to have for dinner each night is a "stressor" in your home, consider creating a weekly menu. Decide on a week's worth of simple dinners, set on a specific day of the week. Make a grocery list of what you need for each meal and then purchase those ingredients.

How to make the change:

We are going to make this simple. We are going to plan for one week. Let's try this approach.....

- Sunday–larger heartier–complete meals
- Monday–casseroles
- Tuesday-soup, salad, and sandwiches
- Wednesday–Italian
- Thursday–chicken something
- Friday–Crockpot cooking
- Saturday–taco or Mexican meal

Let me suggest one very important rule:

Keep all of your recipes simple. Stay away from the ones that have a bunch of ingredients. Save the extravagant meals for a later date. This week think easy. Even though there are many yummy recipes, try to avoid them. It will be much easier.

Sunday—the heartier meal

For this day, usually you are home and can do more prep work. This can be more of a baked meal like whole chicken, Salisbury steak, meatloaf, lasagna, etc.

Monday–casserole

Make your Mondays easy and think casserole day. You can throw pasta or rice with some ground burger and a sauce and make a multitude of different recipes.

Tuesday–soup, salad, sandwiches

Make a simple salad, lettuce with a few vegetables chopped up makes it easy.

Soup is a great "stretcher" dish that you can add all kinds of things to it and make it tasty.

For sandwiches, you can make them simple. Choose a tuna fish melt or a grilled cheese. A wrap with basic meat, vegetables, and dressing. Think easy and simple, something that takes no time to prepare.

Wednesday–Italian

This one is easy, make spaghetti. Need an easy version??? Buy the jarred sauce, pasta, and a pkg of hamburger—-very simple. You can boil some fettuccine noodles and pour some jarred Alfredo sauce over top of. Serve with baked chicken strips.

Thursday–chicken something

Choose one of your family's favorite, EASY chicken dishes.

Friday is Crockpot cooking day

Make the end of your week easy by throwing something in the Crockpot early on in the day.

Saturday–taco or Mexican day

This is also an easy meal to make. You can put out a variety of sides: rice, beans, seasoned meat, lettuce, salsa, cheese, and sour cream. Everyone can make their own creation. Provide tortillas—soft and hard shell. Easy meal!

The goal this week is to make your dinner meals plain and simple. Get rid of the stressful dinner hour in your home and learn to enjoy this time.

Chapter 35

The change: to listen to uplifting Christian music for a week

Music is a powerful source. It has a definite impact on us in most, if not all aspects of our lives. Music can change the mood of a person, act as a carrier for suggestions, and even influence the mind. You can appreciate the power of music by imagining yourself watching your favorite movie without any music or watching commercials being void of music.

I'm sure you have experienced a situation where you happen to hear a certain melody or a particular song on the radio and all types of emotions arise based on past events. That is how we can experience and appreciate the influence that music has on us.

Why make the change:

Music is important to the Christian lifestyle because music influences us much. Therefore, we should be diligent about what type of music we listen to.

Before I was a saved Christian, I listened to worldly music. Music that put me in the mood for sadness, music that put me in a "quirky" kind of mood. It amazes me how much my mood was affected by listening to certain types of music. My depression was deepened as I allowed sad songs to flow. My anger would rage as I listened to "anger-provoking" songs. As much as we don't want to believe it, we ARE influenced by music.

Music influences us and it can set the stage for many things mentally and spiritually. Music can assist us in entering the presence of God. It could be used to change our state of mind and it could be used for mere entertainment. We as Christians should be aware of the impact that music has on us and act accordingly. We should monitor what we allow ourselves and our children to listen to.

If you are constantly putting in negative songs into your ear, that is what is going to flow through your heart and out of your mouth. You want to keep music flowing that is giving you a positive impact throughout the day. Not something that is going to bring you down.

How to make the change:

How do we make this change? It is simple….turn off your local worldly station, turn up your local Christian radio station, and let it play all day long. If you don't have a local radio station tune into the internet and stream it live. There are many choices out there that will give you positive, uplifting songs throughout the day.

You want your focus to be on God.

> *It is good to give thanks unto the Lord, and to sing praised to Your name, O Most High." – Psalms 92:1*

Try this for 1 week. Only let your ears hear Christian music for this time. Notice any changes? Did it encourage you more? Make you a happier person? I don't know how I would get through my day without having some sort of constant presence of positive in the background of my busy life. Try it!

Chapter 36

The change: to learn to say, NO!

The ability to say "no" is a hard one in our society. Everyone likes to be busy doing this and that. They want others to do this for them. We can busy ourselves up all day long by doing requests from everyone else. Sometimes it can get very overwhelming.

The key to learning to simplify our lives starts with us saying, NO. If you can't say NO then you will just keep taking on too many activities, as well as too much stuff. We just need to learn the power of the word–"NO!"

Why make the change:

Do you know that nowhere in the Bible does God say "Thou shalt do everything that everyone asks of you, or you shall perish?" Most of our days are filled with running here or running there. Taking our children to youth groups, cookie sales, soccer practice, and visits with friends. We are busy ourselves running to church meetings, choir practices, and bible studies.

We could practically fill each and every night with some out-of-the home activities. Now don't get me wrong, all those activities are fine, in moderation. When we get so far away from being able to sit and have family dinners, or have walks outside with our children, and just time to sit and reflect with our Father, those are the times when it is time to say "No!"

How to make the change:

Set a night each week that you don't schedule anything but together family home time. Practice saying the word "No," it is quite simple. The next time someone asks you to do something, just say "I'm sorry but I have something on the calendar that day." Be sure to write on your calendar the word "something" so that you are not lying:)

On those scheduled "no days" be sure to do something that has everlasting eternal value. Spend time in God's word, go for a walk with your husband and hold hands, take your little ones outside and run around playing tag, or take your teenagers fishing. Choose things that are relaxing, free from media influence , and things that will bond you together as a family. You will never regret investing quality time with those you love.

Chapter 37

The change: to simplify your eating habits.

How many of us are on "diets" and spend hours counting calories, points, and/or buying expensive meals and bars to "complete" the diet plan? Do you find yourself at the dinner hour frazzled because you "want" to make something healthy, but it is just easier to grab that frozen meal out of the freezer? Have you tried eliminating processed foods, but find that it is too hard to do and resort to packaged meals? Many of these ways are hard to keep up with financially, physically, and mentally.

Do you know that you can eliminate stress and be healthier at the same time just by simplifying your diet? By adopting a plain and simple lifestyle for food WILL help you lose weight, save money, and time.

Why make the change:

The change for a diet that fits into the category for "less stuff more life" is easier than you think. Here are some things you can consider when you go about constructing your simple diet:

- Simple. Everything should be easy to prepare and not take too long. We don't want you to spend hours slaving over the stove. It should take you less than 10 minutes of time to prep the food. Stay away from lots of ingredients.
- Nutritious. Even though our American bodies love junk food, it just makes us fat. Being fat is stressful. We need to be getting fiber, vitamins, minerals, protein, and good fats, into our diets.
- Low in calories, saturated fat, sugar, and cholesterol.

Now that we know what we want to construct our simple diet with, here are some things we want to cut out of our diet:

- Junk food. This is the obvious. Although it can be very tasty, it is simply not healthy for us, and it is usually high

in saturated fat and sugar. Plus a ton of other "bad things."
- Processed food. No fiber, low in nutrition, high in calories. Try to get stuff in its natural state, without all the gravies, sauces, and cheeses on top.
- Fast food. This stuff never comes to any good. You can get a good salad, but it is usually topped with some fried chicken or fatty dressing.
- Red meat. We don't need to completely avoid red meat, but it is high in saturated fat. If you want to eat meat, eat fish, boneless skinless chicken breast, or turkey breast. You can also opt for other forms of protein that doesn't have all the fat: whole grains and beans.
- Fried foods. These types of foods are high in saturated fat and calories. Look for baked, stir fried or even raw.

Now that we have built and weeded out what we can and cannot eat, what do we have left?

Just the basics—-essentials.

If we stock up on those essentials, we can create simple meals that are tasty and easy to prepare. Then by simplifying your eating habits, you not only shorten your prep time, but you save on groceries, and added fat to our bodies which will make us lighter:) I have heard people say that eating processed foods is cheaper, but I don't believe that. You can stock up on basic foods and still provide healthy, nutritious foods for your family at a cheaper price than packaged foods.

How to make the change:

What would a simplified diet look like? It would have a lot of fresh fruits, veggies, beans, nuts, and whole grains.

Here are some simple meals:

Breakfast: Whole-grain cereals (no processed or sugary cereals), oatmeal, fresh homemade bran muffins (use whole-grain flour), homemade granola, fresh fruits, whole-grain toast with butter, and scrambled eggs.

Lunch: Sandwiches such as turkey or avocado with tomatoes and sprouts on whole wheat bread; pita filled with hummus and tomatoes and sprouts and lettuce; leftover soup or chili.

Dinner: Make a big pot of hearty soup that can last for days. You can make cabbage vegetable soup , a minestrone type, or chili. Make a hearty salad with nuts, spinach, avocados, lettuce, carrots and a light dressing. Steamed veggies pair well with seasoned brown rice (use sesame seed oil and soy sauce or tamari.)

Snacks: Fruits, cut-up veggies, nuts, or blue corn chips with salsa.

Treats: Every now and then you need to treat yourself. If you've been good, splurge on something. Just don't make it every day. Maybe once a week if you have eaten well.

Take some of these ideas and implement them this week. If it seems overly complicated, choose one meal and work with that. Change your breakfast eating habits first, then when you have the hang of it, move up to lunch. Continue onward with dinner. Just start with something and get the ball rolling.

Chapter 38

The change: to pay off small debt

How do some people go through life living happy, content, debt free, and completely in control of their finances while others are living in a downward spiral of heavy debt, past due notices, and collection agencies calling every day? The answer is the debt free people have a plan and make it work. They live life content and not on a spur of the moment whim. They look for creative ways to save and put away for that rainy day.

Why make the change:

Most Americans are in debt. A HUGE number in debt. Our creator knew that we should not live in debt....in Proverbs 22:7 says...

> *The rich ruleth over the poor, and the borrower is servant to the lender*

How true is that? Whenever you "owe" someone money, you are constantly feeling the stress and strain of paying back your lender. How much better of a scenario to have consistently saved up your money and you are able to pay cash for your purchases.

How to make the change:

As this is a less stuff more life challenge and the main goal is to SIMPLIFY your life, I encourage you to get rid of things. Have a garage sale, put things up for sale on EBay, or sell things on Craigslist. Have a "get rid of mentality." Don't be adamant about getting a certain price for things, if someone gives you an offer, take it. That money is going to help you better than the item sitting back in your basement. I grow tired of garage sales with price tags, I have to wonder if the people really want to get rid of the items or if they would rather stuff them back into their basements?!?!

Take all the money that you have earned and put it towards paying off a small debt. If you are living debt free, put it towards an emergency fund or special savings. The goal is to get rid of things, make some cash and pay off a small debt. You will feel invigorated and lighter. Free from that financial burden. Plus you will rid your household of some unnecessary items.

Let's say that you are already clutter free in your home and you still want to pay off a small debt, what can you do then? Maybe work a few extra hours each week and take the money earned and put it directly towards your debt. Become debt free and you can fulfill God's law…….

Owe no man anything, but to love one another: for he that loveth another hath fulfilled the law.

Romans 13:8

Chapter 39

The change: a place for everything

We have all heard the old saying, "*a place for everything and everything in its place.*" But how many of us put this into practice? Can you look around right now and see the accumulated clutter on your kitchen counter? Can you open a drawer and find a myriad of miscellaneous junk just sitting there? Has your living room become a "catch-all" for children's toys? Then it is time to put this age old saying into use.

Why make the change:

Okay, let's do a simple test to see if this is something that you should take part in. Without leaving your chair or couch that you are sitting on, can you answer the following questions:

- Do you know where your car keys are?
- Do you know where your phone charger is?
- Do you know where your 2015 tax papers are?
- Do you know where your social security card is?
- Do you know where your winter gloves are?
- Do you know where the bug spray from last summer is at?
- Do you know where last season's shoes are located at and if anyone needs new ones?

How did you do?

For many of us, we probably only really care about two of them—the keys and phone charger. Everything else we will spend hours hunting down. But it doesn't have to be this way. Wouldn't it be nicer to know that you have a place established for everything and that with a quick look, you will be able to access it?

How to make the change:

This is something that you do, AFTER you declutter your home. It doesn't make sense to keep throwing things in places when you FIRST need to declutter and get rid of items.

Here are some simple steps to helping you find a place for everything:

1. Take a look around your home and every item that is lying around visibly. Now think of a logical place for each item. Some items you will put with other similar stuff. Maybe it is your husband's wallet, keys, and loose change, find a small container and put all of his items together in an accessible spot, ready to grab when headed out the door.
2. Ideally before you find a place for something, think long and hard whether or not you really need the object in question. Ask yourself, "Have I used this item at ALL in the last year?" If you are having a hard time finding a place for items, consider getting rid of it.
3. Repeat, repeat, repeat. This exercise needs to be done over and over again. People wonder why I organize monthly...it is because we accumulate items, and if those items are not dealt with, we will suddenly be thrust into the materialistic world of STUFF. If I notice that my home is become too much to pick up, or that the certain place where I store my ? is constantly getting messed up, then it is time to purge. Time to give up some things.

Want to simplify your life, so that you can have more time to spend with family, more time to spend on self, more time to spend time doing what it is you like to do?? Then spend less time searching for things. Find a place for everything and keep it that way.

Chapter 40

The change: to learn how to unwind from a stress filled day

No matter what kind of life you have, simple or complicated, it all comes with STRESS! From being a stay at home Mom with a toddler, to a multi millionaire CEO of a company—they have two things in common—-they both experience STRESS.

Why make the change:

No matter how simplified our lives are, things in life happen. Babies cry, people will let us down, friends will let us down, dinner will burn, money will be tight, the car will break down, and our husbands will let us down occasionally. It is part of life. There is no way to avoid it. Nothing that we can do will prevent it. It just happens, it is called LIFE. But knowing what you can do to help yourself unwind after a stressful day is important in saving your sanity, your heart, and your peace of mind.

How to make the change:

Next time, when everything seems to just fall apart, try some of these ways to unwind from stress:

- Take a few deep breaths. Sometimes when my children are driving me crazy and I want to yell, I stop and take a few deep breaths. Breathing in, holding it, and then slowly letting it out. Sometimes it helps to do this 3-5 times as needed.
- Do a self massage. When tensions run high, give yourself a neck rub. Rub your head, massaging your scalp to release tension . If you have a great massaging husband or child, let them do it for you.
- Take a walk. When life gets unbearable and you feel like you can't go anymore without exploding, get away. Take a walk and breathe deeply, letting go of the worries of the stress. Even if it is for 5 minutes, just to get out and get a chance to regroup will make a difference.

- Take a day off. For some of us, this won't be possible. But if you are having a hard time with the children, let your spouse know that you are needing some time away. Grab something to eat and go sit somewhere relaxing all by yourself and give yourself time to regroup.
- If you aren't a stay at home Mom, then spend time with your family. Nothing is better than reminding yourself why it is your doing what you do at work—-you are doing it for your children and spouse.
- Unwire yourself from media. Shut off your phone, avoid emails, and avoid the television. Just learn to shut your brain off for a few hours. Constantly worrying about emails, status's, or even stress of sites not loading up quickly, are enough to stress you out. Get away from it, go take a walk in nature, take your family to the park, and learn to unwind.
- Take a nap. Nothing can cure stress more quickly than by taking a much needed rest. Just a 20 minute cat nap will help you deal more effectively with the stress.

Learning to implement just a few of these steps each day, will help ensure some peace into your daily life.

Chapter 41

The change: get back to God

Having children has reminded me of how spiritually irresponsible we can become if we are not careful. We need the basics of getting back to God.

How many parents out there have to continually remind your child to do the basic daily tasks of the day…..brush your teeth, make your bed, and pick up your dirty laundry? Sometimes we as adults, are just as irresponsible in our daily life with the basics of getting back to God.

Why make the change:

The basics of knowing who God is include:

1. Knowing Jesus Christ as my personal Savior. One of the first verses my children are taught at church is John 3:16 which says:

For God so loved the world, that he gave his only begotten Son, that whosoever believeth in him should not perish, but have everlasting life.

They are also taught from a young age the *Plan of Salvation*. They make it basic and simple, like God does ….ABC

A——Admit: Confess to God that you are a sinner. Repent or turn away from your sin.

B—Believe: Trust that Jesus is God's Son and that God sent Jesus to save people from their sins.

C—Commit: Give your life to Jesus. Ask Him to be your Lord and Savior.

2. Reading the Bible and praying EVERYDAY.

Paul repeatedly encourages the early church to study and pray without ceasing. If you ask most people why they don't pray and study the bible daily, the number one excuse will be NO TIME. But in life, we make time for the things we deem important.

We need to evaluate our lives and ask ourselves how pleasing would the Lord be with our idle or "free time?" How much time do we spend on the phone, texting, or viewing online social media places? How easy is it to turn to God when things get rough or we "NEED" him to help with something? Do we turn to Him when we arise in the morning and thank Him for the blessings in our life? It shouldn't be about all of the wants and needs we require in life. It should be about Him and thanking and praising Him.

3. Going to church regularly.

I know many people believe in home church, some are just tired of the local church and all the drama, and others get offended because of their own wants out of life. But how important it is for us as believers to be encouraged and fellowship regularly with other believers.

It is important to do as God says, and rest on the Sabbath day. Take the time to devote it and praise Him. What a glorious time in heaven it must be on Saturday-in some cases and Sunday- when the Lord is receiving praises from His people. It gives you an encouraging time when hearing the message. Time to clear your mind and let God speak to you. It is a spiritual renewing when you are able to engage in worship and feel Gods holy anointing. Many powerful things can happen when bound with a body of believers.

Hebrews 10:25 says....

Not forsaking the assembling of ourselves together, as the manner of some is; but exhorting one another: and so much the more, as ye see the day approaching.

Take this illustration of a mother who labors and works endlessly to prepare a nutritious meal for her children. She carefully plans, shops, and prepares this meal to provide proper nourishment for her children's physical growth. What happens when her children decide not to show up for dinner? One is too busy and grabs a hamburger fast food style, the other one grabs a power bar because it "says it is healthy", the third child decides to eat later and will "reheat' the leftovers only to discover that they are gone when he was hungry.

Now flip this to a pastor who carefully plans, organizes, and prepares their message for their "flock of sheep." What if some don't come because they are too tired, they have a ball game, or just don't want to go because someone snubbed them the wrong way? Where are they going to get their spiritual nourishment from?

How important it is for us parents to set an example for our children. What are our attitudes and lack of consistency saying to our children and to the future generations of our world?

Some may argue that there isn't as much time in our weeks as the early church was portrayed in the Bible. They got together continually to do the Lords' service. Yes, times have changed, but have those times changed for the better?

What are we putting in our lives to be priority instead of putting God first? Are sports, work, or time in front of the TV, robbing us of time we could be investing in God? What things do we value? What things in our life do we spend money on the most, are they for lasting things or temporary happiness?

4. Encouraging other believers.

Iron sharpeneth iron; so a man sharpeneth the countenance of his friend.

Proverbs 27:17

Bear ye one another's burdens, and so fulfill the law of Christ.

Galatians 6:2

As believers it is important that we encourage our brothers and sisters in the Lord. Especially when we know that they are going through a struggle. We must do as Jesus would do and that is to love others, unconditionally.

How to make the change:

In life some things are more easily said than done, but with this "back to God" it is rather simple. No matter what the situation, you can still do most ALL of the above. It doesn't take much to read the scriptures, pray, and encourage one another. While you are waiting on your husband or financial situations to change, start praying to God asking Him for wisdom and direction in your life. Continually thank Him for the blessings in life and keep reading scriptures to help Him speak to you.

Anyone can get back to the basics of God, it just takes a decision to do it. I encourage you to reevaluate your priorities in life, today, right now.

Chapter 42

The change: to edit your commitments

Could you imagine if we were able to "edit our lives?" Think of all the things that we would just be able to erase out of them:

- negative people
- meaningless time spent doing absolutely nothing
- commitments that we signed up for, but are quickly taking over our life by imposing on our time spent with family and those we love
- taking back all of those things that were once important to us but have simply just become obsolete in our lives

Why make the change:

Each and every time you make a commitment in your life, it leaves less and less room for doing those things which are important to you. You need to take inventory of all of your commitments and start editing them.

The reason people don't cut or "edit their commitments" is because it leads to feelings of guilt. How are they going to look to friends, co-workers, the church staff, or the school PTA if they decide to "cut" that commitment? How are others going to count on you and who will they turn to, to do that job?

Trust me, there will ALWAYS be another person willing to fill in the gaps.

First thing you need to do, is not feel guilty. You need to realize what a HUGE relief NOT having to do that commitment each day or week or month is going to do for you. It WILL free up much of your time, even though others may be disappointed, you can't go through life pleasing EVERYONE else according to their plan. You have to do what works for you and your family.

If we committed to what everyone else wanted ALL of the time, we would never have any time left for ourselves. This is not much of a life to lead.

How to make the change:

First start with making a list. Make a list of ALL of the commitments that you have in your life. Here are some areas to consider:

- Work, you may have many commitments at your employment, list all of them.
- Home, aside from family/children commitments you also have commitments at home to take care of.
- Family, you may be the role of mother, wife, daughter, aunt, etc these all come with many commitments.
- Children, your children may have many activities that they are committed to, list them.
- Home business, you may have a small business at home, list commitments to that.
- Religious/Civic, you may volunteer for different organizations, or be part of church teachings or attending church activities, commitments.
- Hobbies–you might have groups for hobbies, like book clubs, fishing groups, etc, these all come with commitments.
- Online, you may have commitments to meet online, list those.

Now that you have your "list," take a close look at each thing on it. Consider the following:

- Does this give value to my life or my family's life?
- How important is this to me?
- Does this line up with my priorities and values?
- How is my life affected if I drop out?
- Does this further the goals I have in life?

Some of these are going to be tough questions to answer, but I hope that if you can eliminate the ones that give you the least amount of return on your invested time and effort, you will be better for it. If there are any that do not line up with your life goals and priorities, cut them out.

If you are afraid of cutting out things, then I suggest that you do them for a few weeks. Cut it out, see how your life is without them. Is it something that you miss? Something that you are glad to be done with? Something that you don't even think about? This isn't a forever list, you can drop things and add them back as needed.

I guarantee that your family life, your relationship with your husband/wife will be much better when you can learn to say NO to commitments and start enjoying life together as one.

Chapter 43

The change: to simplify your clothing

When I had visited some of the Amish homes I noticed something right away. These women wore a very basic style dress. They had an assortment of different patterns and colors but only one style. Their stockings were one color, their shoes one color. "Hmmmm, making your wardrobe simplistic, now there is an idea."

Why make the change:

Having a simple wardrobe means that you can:

- Enjoy everything you wear, everyday.
- Have an easier time picking an outfit in the morning.
- Feel refreshed instead of burdened or overwhelmed when you open your closet.

How to make the change:

I know there are many different ways to simplify your closet, this is how I do it myself. For those of you that don't like plain and simple, this might not work for you. Those ready for a change, I challenge you to try this way.

- Pick a staple color as your base wardrobe color. Mine is brown.
- Keep your undershirts the same color. I wear layers of clothing for modesty reasons. I almost always have on a undershirt. I have about four brown colored t-shirts to wear under my outfits.
- For bottoms, I have many solid color skirts–brown, jean, and khaki. I do have some stylish skirts and the main color is brown.
- My dresses have browns in them. When I am shopping I look for those colors and know that I already have an undershirt to go with. When I keep my theme color-- brown, I know I can mix and match things easily.

- For my summer wardrobe, I spice it up a bit and add other colors to my wardrobe, such as orange and navy.
- For shoes, I keep them one color. Brown boots and brown sandals. Simple.
- For socks, I keep them black. I should go brown, but haven't found them yet. All the same, no worries about unmatched pairs, because they are either ankle socks or knee highs.

By keeping my wardrobe with a staple color has helped me tremendously when shopping because I know what I am looking for and that it will pretty much go with what I have at home. Simple, basic, and easy.

Chapter 44

The change: to learn calmness in ALL situations in life

Remaining positive no matter what life throws at you, is hard. How many times per day are we "attacked" by a negative person? What about negative situations or ones that bring about stress or frustration? What about with relationships of close people that bring drama and upset to your life ? We ALL have experienced this, no one is exempt from it. But what if we could respond to any of these situations with a state of peace and not anger? Where we could walk away from it and not "stew" over the anger inside. Imagine couples that do not stay angry for days on end. Families who don't grow bitter towards one another. It sometimes can sound too unreal. In reality this is feasible, with the right approach.

Why make the change:

I think we all know or should know the effects of negative stress in our life. High stress levels lead to heart disease, depression, and obesity. Focusing on the negative thing in our life will only lead us further into a life of despair. We need to focus on the positive things in our lives. We also need to realize that life happens. Bad things happen. People are generally unhappy, angry individuals and sometimes you are going to get caught in the cross roads. Your best bet is to learn to be calm. Choose to be positive and calm when faced with a negative in life.

How to make the change:

How do we go about making the change to calmness in ANY and ALL situations in life?

- Learn to pray. If we can learn to give away our worries and frustrations to God, that can be the first step to bringing peace of mind and a better perspective to having calmness in life.
- Learn to detach. When faced with a negative situation where your first response is anger, detach yourself.

Think about the situation as a whole, instead of just the tiny part that is affecting you. You look at all of the different facets of the problem and view them as an observer without judgment.
- Take a breather. If you find yourself getting angry or emotionally upset over an issue, take a step back and take a few breaths. Sometimes that will mean you have to tell a person, that you need a minute and will be right back. Get yourself together and come back ready to respond in a positive light. If it is an email or text, let it sit, take a few moments to breathe and then respond.
- Let things roll off of you. Realize that people who are angry and rude have bad days. Their problems do not have to be yours. If someone is mean, you don't have to be mean back. Sometimes the best response is a smile. The Bible talks about "reaping coals of fire" on our enemies. If we don't respond negatively to people, but do in a positive light, it is like reaping coals of fire on someone's head.
- Get some understanding. If someone says something mean to you, instead of taking it personally, understand that you are not the center of this person's world. You just happen to be the target of their frustration. They could be having a bad day, having marital problems, frustrated in their own walk with God, or maybe even not understanding the issue very well.

People ALWAYS have a reason for anger and rudeness. If you can understand what is the core of that, it is much easier to deal with. Be the better person and experience calmness when faced with any situation in your life.

Chapter 45

The change: to subtract people/things that deduct from your life

Okay, we ALL have them….people and things that take WAY too much unnecessary time from our lives. It may be time spent finding out what is going on online. It may be long, negative phone conversations spent with friends, or it could be sitting in front of the television watching the "new" series that came out. We all have things in our life that are basically "deducting" from precious time that could be spent in a more positive area.

Why make the change:

How many of us "wish" that we had more time to do things?

I know I make excuses from time to time that say, "If only I had more time….. or I would but I can't seem to fit it into my day." Then some of my "free" time is spent "relaxing" in front of the TV or spent sitting listening to people complain about life.

Now nothing is WRONG with talking and encouraging friends that may be going through a rough time, or even watching a show. I am talking about the things that are constantly time consuming, drain us of emotional energy, and are generally not a "positive" light in our life.

It is easy to keep adding friends and things into our life. We are constantly handed new opportunities to minister, new friends that seem generally okay to hang out with, and many commitments that sound like great opportunities for our children. But not everything NEEDS to be added to our life.

If you are finding that you are emotionally drained after visiting with a friend, stressed out trying to get to prior commitments, and most importantly your spouse does not view your friends or your desire to fill your schedules full as good, it is then time to subtract things.

How to make the change:

I know myself, I have had people come into my life that are generally not adding benefits to it. Not that people have to "add" but you can get wrapped up in "saving" people or letting them unleash their problems more times than needed. It is a fine line and something that needs to be put through to God first.

These people could be family, best friends, or even co-workers. If you are finding that the majority of your time with these people results in negative behavior it may be time to subtract. It may be because of their lifestyle choices, or maybe they constantly like to complain and bring negativity into your life. Whatever the reason, if this results in you being negative yourself, it is time to deduct.

Now, we can't always just drop people, although some may beg to differ. You can subtract people from your life without severing all ties. Sometimes it can mean less time talking to them, or finding other avenues that you can pour your time into like say time with your children.

Sometimes it is commitments and a full schedule that need to be subtracted from our lives. I know when I fill my days and barely have time to sit and talk with my husband each evening, he gets frustrated. If I am running around here and there not being a "keeper at home" then how can I show my children the value of what God has called me to be? Activities are fun to do, don't get me wrong, but you have to find that balance of what is God-honoring and family-honoring.

You shouldn't be going through life on the hamster wheel, constantly running here and there because you are going to miss some really great things that only come from having some quiet, relaxing time. Your children, your spouse, and you, deserve to be able to enjoy just doing nothing but being with each other.

I want my children to learn that you don't always have to be doing something to be happy. I want them to value friendships in the way that it is better to have a few really good ones then lots of broken, stressed out, emotional taking ones.

The best ways to decide which people, commitments, or activities to subtract from your life is to seek God in prayer. Ask Him to show you which ones are taking from your life in a negative way. Go to your husband and ask him if there are any activities, people, or commitments that he sees as unhealthy in your life.

That could be a hard thing to do. We are generally people pleasers and to feel like you let someone down will be hard to do. But life is too short, we need to be adding positive things and people to our life not keeping the ones that deduct from it.

Chapter 46

The change: to get rid of the "bad" stuff from our diets.

Most all of us when we realize that we need to "lose a few pounds" immediately step into "diet" mode and start eliminating things from our diet. We are often left hungry, moody, and look for every quick weight loss scam out there which in turn leaves us financially lighter. We "ban" ourselves from eating foods that are good for us in an attempt to shed a few pounds. Sometimes we lose them and then we immediately return to our old ways and the cycle continues.

Why make the change:

The key to success in long term weight loss is to make changes that will stick. We need to reprogram our brain to a completely different way of eating. We have been falsely led to believe that everything in the store is good for us. Even if the label says "natural" we think that it is good for us.

That is not the case.

We need to be eating food that is found mostly in its natural state. Sometimes this may sound overwhelming and expensive, but it doesn't have to be. The key to changing our lifestyle diet to a more basic, simple one is to get rid of processed things one food at a time.

How to make the change:

When you think of changing your diet, picture returning your diet to a basic one. Think, "what would you do if there was no local store to buy your packaged food?" What would you serve for dinner tonight? You want to return to a diet where you can buy things in bulk and eat off of them for a long time. Think rice, dried beans, whole wheat flour, and popcorn seeds.

When I purchased my first bulk buy of those items, for the most part they sat in my basement only slowly getting used. I enjoyed buying snack mix instead of making popcorn for snacks. Oatmeal wasn't as appealing as cold cereal. Dried beans?? Those took too much time to make, I wanted canned ones.

I then had to do things slowly. I made a list. A list of how I wanted to rid our foods of packaged, processed foods and return to a more whole foods centered diet.

Here was our list:

1. eliminate white flour, sugar, bread, and pasta
2. replace sugary drinks and sodas with water
3. avoid packaged foods with more than 5 ingredients
4. replace fake margarine's and vegetable oils with real butter and olive/coconut oils
5. replace table salt with sea or Himalayan salt
6. replace snack foods with fresh fruit or veges
7. stop eating out and start making meals
8. work on replacing a few items in my pantry each month that I buy as a "convenience food". Example–canned beans, taco seasoning, ranch mix, etc.
9. make most of my grocery budget go to fresh fruits and vegetables

Did we make these changes overnight? No we slowly worked on them. It took about a year to complete this list.

I am realizing the impact food has on my children's health as well as their temperament. I realize that we have more energy, don't feel as sluggish halfway through the day, and feel fuller longer if I am wise in choosing good foods. This results in less snacking from the more nutrient dense foods they eat.

I used to believe in 3 meals a day with 2-3 snacks but I realize that when I feed my children "real" foods they can go much longer and feel fuller longer periods of time throughout the day.

It has been a slow journey but with each new choice, it takes some time getting used to and then it usually sticks. I have found that it takes 5-10 times of offering new foods to my child before they even eat it. I myself used to despise trail mix. I thought it was gross. Now it has become my new favorite snack food for the day. Everything takes time. It takes time to reprogram our taste buds to something more basic and simple. Thus the reason for this challenge, if you can start by changing one new thing a week or month, then it's better than not beginning at all.

Chapter 47

The change : to challenge yourself

There is much reference online to making a "bucket" list for the summer and a bucket list to do before you reach a certain age and I was always thinking to myself, "Why do people need a bucket list to get things done?" I realized I challenge myself on a weekly basis and my life is basically a bucket list. Not many people think like I do and that is okay, thus the reason for a bucket list.

Why make the change:

I am not encouraging you to go and make a list of things like swimming with dolphins, go skydiving, etc. But what is wrong with making a list that pertains to challenging our own life and making it better? Why should we "settle" for being a mom who doesn't know how to cook, one who doesn't have a green thumb, or maybe one who has problems communicating in her marriage?

We should be striving as women to be the best that we can be.

Striving to better ourselves will improve our quality of life. It may save you some money, and could enhance those lives of people around you.

What are some things that prevent people from challenging their life?

Fear

Fear of failure, fear of going out of their comfort zone, and fear of the unknown.

Over-thinking

People start over analyzing things and start making a mountain out of a mole hole. Just take things one step at a time.

Not recognizing achievement

They fail to see how far they have come and look instead, to how far they have to go

Learn from it

As with everything learn from your mistakes, take what you would do differently and don't be afraid to try again.

How to make the change:

This part is easy, start by making a list of things you want to improve upon in your life. Examples include:

- learn how to bake homemade bread
- learn how to sew
- learn how to garden
- learn how to be a good listener-by keeping mouth shut
- share talents with someone–example teach sewing to neighbor girls
- cut my food budget by 50%
- make all foods from scratch
- organize my paper mess
- organize my household
- make a budget and stick to it
- make some extra income–brainstorm ways

There are many different things you can do and with everyone it is a different story. I encourage you to improve and challenge yourself and ways. You will be a better person by stretching yourself and your comfort level.

Our greatest glory is not in never failing, but in rising every time we fall.

Confucius

Chapter 48

The change: to avoid materialism

In our society we are fueled by consumption. We are constantly bombarded with media ads, newspaper ads, magazine ads, television commercials, ads on our apps, the list goes on and on. Having more and more things doesn't necessarily make us happier, contrary to what society is telling us.

Living a less materialistic lifestyle doesn't mean that we are to move to Alaska in a cabin and disappear from society. What it does mean is that we shift our focus away from possessions so that they become less important.

Why make the change:

We hunger for more in life. We want more money, more power, more success, more gizmos. We live for it. We are constantly thinking what we would do when we make the next amount of money to buy such and such a thing. It never ends. We forget about the things that we already have because we are constantly looking at the things that we don't have yet.

What motivates a person to want more? Our society tells us that by having more things we will be:

- happier
- secure
- important

How to make the change:

How do we go about making the change to resist materialism when our society is jamming it down our throats?

Resist....Rejoice....Refocus....Return

1. We **resist** comparing ourselves to what other people have.

2. We **rejoice** in what we do have and be thankful for it.
3. **Refocus** on things that really matter and count.
4. **Return** to God. Focusing our happiness, our security, and realizing our worth can only come from God.

Here is a thought? What is the opposite of materialism?

Giving. Is it safe to say that the antidote to materialism is giving? It means the exact opposite of getting. The Bible instructs us to tithe. Tithing is an act of worship. Each time you give, you are winning the war on materialism. When you pay your tithe, you are putting your faith and trust in God to provide for your security and to take care of your needs. What about your offering? Do you seek God to show you in what areas that you need to give money to help grow the Kingdom of God? What about paying alms? Do you give to the poor, the widowed, the orphans? These are all ways in which we can give financially to help others. Don't store up treasures on this earth. Invest in people, in lives, and in things that are going to help others while here in this lifetime.

Chapter 49

The change: to establish routines

How many of us moms, can go about our day and later on question, if you remembered to brush your toddlers teeth that morning? Or you may wonder if the dog got fed today?

How easy it can be to forget the simplest of tasks because you fail to have a routine set for every morning and evening.

Why make the change:

Every family needs routines. Routines help us to organize life, give it a sense of purpose, plus cut down on the chaos because people know what to expect.

Having routine helps maintain a sense of peace and order in our life. If we know that each morning we have A, B, and C to do, then we do it without thinking. If we expect our children to get A,B, and C done before they can go off and play, that makes morning time much more stress free when trying to establish some routines. It allows you the parent to not have to constantly "nag" your child to get certain tasks done. Plus, they get done without arguments or questions.

How to make the change:

How do you go about making new routines? You begin by making a list. You make a list of things you want to accomplish yourself in the morning and evening.

You then can make lists for your children of the different tasks you want them to complete before school.

Be specific. Here is my sample morning routine list:

- wake up/shower/get ready
- drink a glass of water

- have a cup of coffee
- have personal devotion time
- quick wipe the bathrooms
- throw in a load of laundry
- make breakfast
- wake up children
- eat and take vitamin
- clean up kitchen and wash dishes
- Begin day…..

Do a similar one for nighttime:

- do a quick pick up of house
- feed/water animals
- make sure breakfast prep is ready
- fill coffee pot with water
- read a book instead of watching a movie to fall asleep to

These are just samples, yours will fit your lifestyle. I know that personally when my children have some order in their lives they are much better behaved. They know what they have to do and they get it done. There isn't nagging from Mom, they know what is expected. It gives them a sense of accomplishment.

Print your list off and place it in an area to see. You can also make checklists for your children to check off each time they complete a tasks. This helps give them more accountability to get things done. Plus it will free you from exerting energy on unnecessary delegating. As it is already done.

Chapter 50

The change: to declutter a room

Do you ever feel that when you look around your room it is like you are living in chaos? Do you ever feel overwhelmed with the amount of work that it takes to keep up in your rooms? When looking for things, does it take hours to search for them because there is much to sift through in your rooms? If you have answered, YES to any of these questions then this challenge is definitely for you.

Why make the change:

Simplifying or decluttering a room can sometimes be overwhelming. The amount of stuff that you have in your life along with all the things that you have to do can seem like an enormous mountain which you are unable to climb. But guess what? It is NOT something that you need to tackle in one day. It is not something that you have to tackle alone. I want you, to pick and choose which areas of your life are overwhelming to you and start simplifying them to bring you peace and contentment in your days. It all starts with one thing at a time. This challenge is just to declutter one room.

How to make the change:

Decluttering is best when taking in small steps. For example, just do one drawer or one closet, but this challenge is for those that want to do an entire room in one sweep. I want you to pretend that your room is a clock. Pick the noon time and start there. Continue moving around your room in a clock pattern until you end up at your starting point. During this clock momentum, I want you to go through the items in that time zone.

Work with one drawer or one shelf at a time. Here is how you declutter:

1. Dump entire contents of drawer or shelf in a small work area.
2. Next decide, immediately what is trash and throw that away.
3. Grab items that do not belong in this area to be put in their proper place
4. Sort through items and decide immediately if they are a keep or a discard. If you have to give it a second thought then just get rid of it. More than likely you will never need it.
5. Items that have not been used in 6 months, will more than likely not get used.
6. Wipe out drawers and shelves with proper cleaning tools.
7. Place items back in drawers or on shelf.
8. Continue this way until all areas have been cleaned.

When finished, decide which items to give away to people and sort into plastic bags or boxes. Place near an area so that they do not get overlooked to deliver to them. Throw trash away immediately, not giving you a second chance to keep it.

Working this way, you should be done in 1-2 hours. If the room is really cluttered than maybe 3-5 hours.

When finished, sit back and enjoy a peaceful setting. You will be glad what you did.

Chapter 51

The change: Learn to let go

Letting go is hard, but sometimes holding on is harder.

Why is it, that we hold onto our pain far beyond its ability to serve us? It's like we create and maintain problems because they give us a sense of identity about who we are or who we want to stay as.

We will replay past mistakes and failures over and over again in our heads. We allow feelings of shame and regret to shape our actions in the present. We will cling to frustration and worry about the future as if that is going to do something for us. We hold stress in our minds and bodies, potentially creating serious health issues, and accept that state of tension as the norm.

Because why? We can't learn to let go.

Why make the change:

"Letting go" can mean a multitude of things to different people. It can mean:

Letting go and not worrying about my house being cleaned perfectly so that I can enjoy fellowship with a friend that stops over for the afternoon.

Letting go and not keeping up appearances because I am afraid of what I will look like to others.

Letting go and not "making" my husband conform to my wants. Example, him not wearing his shoes in my house, eating the foods that I choose, or not leaving his clothing where he wants.

Letting go of my older teenagers and allowing them to grow on their own.

Letting go of my past hurt and allowing myself to grow.

Letting go of my expectations as a Mom and what I am called to be doing.

Letting go of controlling different situations in my life—finances, spouse, children, job, or friends.

Letting go and surrendering my life to the Lord.

There are many different aspects that we ALL struggle and deal with on a daily basis. We need to be recognizing what areas in our life we are "holding" onto and learning to let them go and be free.

How to make the change:

Letting go and moving on, isn't always easy. Here are some things you can do to help ease the process:

1. **Accept and be thankful**. It is what it is. People are people and you can't do anything about it. Be thankful for the memories, hold onto the good ones and get rid of the bad ones. Every situation and problem has value, learn from it and move forward taking positive steps to avoid it.
2. **Focus on change**. Realize that not everything in life is meant to be understood. You can drive yourself crazy mulling over the could of, should of, would of, statements in your head. Realize that bad things happen and to good people. You just have to live, let go, and learn what you can from it. Don't waste energy worrying about the things you can't change. Focus on what you CAN change. If there appears to be nothing that you can change, than change the way you think about it.
3. **Stop playing the victim.** Playing the victim feels good. People like the "poor me syndrome." They enjoy the attention they get from it. Guess what? That gets old quickly. Yes, your feelings do matter, but don't think that the world owes you for your problems. Everyone has them, it is part of life, we get knocked down and then get back up. Take ownership of the problem, you be responsible for your happiness and outcome in life. Don't let someone else decide that for you.

4. **Forgiveness**. In every moment of the day, you have a choice. A choice to continue to feel bad about another person's actions, or the choice to start feeling good. You need to take responsibility for your own happiness, and not put such power into the hands of another. Make the choice to forgive and move on.
5. **Get rid of excess.** You need to rid yourself of superfluous excess in your life. Look around your home, in those dark, dusty corners and cupboards. They are filled to the brim with excess stuff. Then start looking at the more difficult items that no longer add value to our lives. Things like sentimental items, our unnecessarily large home, the expensive toys and gadgets, and bad relationships. Start asking yourself what purpose does this serve in my life?

You have the power to decide whether you want to be happy and move forward with your life or if you want to try to hang onto all of those "excessive" things that will ultimately be too heavy for you to carry and will cause you to stumble in some shape or form.

"Letting go" means learning from those negative experiences and realizing that you don't have to take all of it with you as you try and move forward. Take the lessons and move onward. Sometimes it is an expectation that you have with something and you just have to say, "Okay, it's not for me to decide how things SHOULD go, I have to just do and let everything fall into place in time. Let go of expectations. Be content. Be happy.

Chapter 52

The change: to make small gradual changes

Some wise words from Martin Luther King :

"You don't have to see the whole staircase, just take the first step."

How true that is for our challenge this year of "less stuff more life." I have written about 52 small changes that you can make to help simplify your lifestyle. Most people that you talk to WANT to make changes to their current lifestyle but most find it difficult to do. They start looking at the entire picture of what they want in their life, whether it be a better body, change of diet, a cleaner house, more organized life, or a better personal relationship within themselves. But instead of looking at the entire picture and getting overwhelmed they need to just take a step. Just one. Taking one small step towards a larger goal is better than not taking any step at all.

Why make the change:

We have been giving this great life that we live. We need to live it. We should stop being in the rut of daily hum drum tasks and just do it. Stop making excuses. Trust me, I have been one that has done that. My excuses these last few years are:

- I was too tired
- I am too busy
- I will worry about that later on

But guess what?? Later on will never come. You will ALWAYS be too busy. We can throw a million different things into our days, but we NEED to decide which things are worth pursuing to be most effective in our days. You will probably always be too tired as well, but it doesn't take much of working on our goal even if it is for twenty minutes a day.

One of our families favorite quotes is by Henry David Thoreau and it is true for most people in life:

Most men lead lives of quiet desperation and go to the grave with the song still in them.

How many of us have big dreams that we only DREAM about in our life? Most everyone does. It is the very few that actually go forward and make strides to attain these goals.

How to make the change:

How do we go about making these changes? We all have a resistance to making a change. Why go AGAINST the flow when it seems you are just sailing along?

Take small steps

Instead of going from point A to point D in one full swoop, because you can, go from point A to point B. It is much easier to start small in our changes then making drastic ones. A person can get used to gradual changes much better than one who jumps right in and then sometimes jumps right back out because it was overwhelming.

That is why we start small. Gradually start working your way up.

Finding joy

In order for anyone to stick to something they need to find JOY in doing it. For myself, I despise exercising. I do not like to do it at all. Sweating, doing mundane tasks like running are just not what I enjoy. I have done it, but it has been very easy for me to step back and not do it as much as I would have liked to. I had to change my mode and do something that makes me enjoy exercising. For myself, I include my husband or children. We go to the park and walk the bike path or my little ones and I will dance and do exercises in the living room together. Whatever I can do to make it more enjoyable is what is going to keep me motivated in doing it. Maybe it is seeing that counter space clean in the morning that will motive you to want to keep going organizing your home. We are all different, we ALL need to find the joy that makes us happy.

Keeping it part of your daily routine

Remember you can make tons of changes and see great things happen in your life and then suddenly you gain back 10 pounds, or you start buying processed foods, or that shelf starts accumulating junk again. To integrate change into your life, it needs to become part of your normal everyday routine. If you desire to stay fit, then make sure that every day after dinner you walk. Maybe you desire to pray more, set aside a time specifically like after you shower and before your morning coffee that you do it. It is like having a trigger for you to remember when to do it. The more times that you routinely do the tasks and are reminded by your "trigger" the easier it will become part of your normal everyday life.

 Lastly, remember that you will fail. I say this lightly. Know that you are human and you are going to make mistakes, you will slip up. Using failure as a stepping stone and building upon it for the next try will make all the difference. We learn from failures, we learn how to not do that again and do better the next time.

Authors note:

I pray you have been motivated to WANT to make some changes to your current lifestyle. I hope you seek to live a life filled with less stuff so that you can have more life. For myself, it was the only way that I could achieve a life filled with joy. By eliminating out things that did not add to my life, I was then able to achieve peace and happiness. Life still gets crazy, things go wrong, but by having less stuff filling my time and life with, I am then able to enjoy and have more life. We all deserve a happier life and that begins by making one small change. You have to start the change. Begin today.

Be blessed on your journey to "less stuff more life,"

Amy

Made in the USA
Monee, IL
08 September 2022